# The Least You Can Do Is Be Magnificent

Selected & New Writings, 1983-2016

# The Least You Can Do Is Be Magnificent

Selected & New Writings, 1983-2016

Steve Venright

Compiled & with an afterword by Alessandro Porco

AN IMPRINT OF ANVIL PRESS

"a feed dog book" for Anvil Press

Imprint editor: Stuart Ross
Cover design: Rayola Graphics
Interior design & typesetting: Stuart Ross
Emblems & variegraph: Steve Venright
feed dog logo: Catrina Longmuir
Author photo: Kerry Zentner


Library and Archives Canada Cataloguing in Publication

Venright, Steve
[Poems.  Selections]
     The least you can do is be magnificent : selected & new
writings / Steve Venright.

ISBN 978-1-77214-102-3 (softcover)

     I. Title.

PS8593.E58A6 2017          C811'.54          C2017-906613-7

Printed and bound in Canada

Represented in Canada by Publishers Group Canada
Distributed by Raincoast Books

The publisher gratefully acknowledges the financial assistance of the
Canada Council for the Arts, the Canada Book Fund, and the Province
of British Columbia through the B.C. Arts Council and the Book
Publishing Tax Credit.

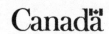

*For Dale Zentner*
*whom I'll love beyond time*
*and through the worlds*

"Let's get this show on the road."
—*the dying words
of Frank Hamilton Lesh*

# Contents

**Part Two**

*Floors of Enduring Beauty and Other Fine Quality Realities
(2000-2016)*

# Lighting the Towers (Author's Foretext)

It is with the loftiest breed of satisfaction, dear Readers—Friends and Colleagues, Obliging Relations, Long-Lost Strangers, Fellow Explorers, Resonators Familiar and Unknown, Mystery Scholars, Bookworms and Nightscrawlers, Illustrious Critics, Logophiles and Literary Thrill-Seekers, Students with Weird Teachers, Library Ghosts and other Bibliovoyeurs, Undercover Shoppers, Time Travellers from the Future and Past, Transdimensional Immigrants, Remote Viewers Wherever You Are, Hollow-Earth Refugees, Extratellurian Vacationers and Interstellar Emissaries, Precocious Housecats, Hybrid Lemurs, Lucid Dreamers, Torpor Vigilantes, Children of the Turbulation, *Fleurs du Mal*, Hunters of the Snark, Bouzingos, 'Pataphysicians, Dadaists, Surrealists, Angelheaded Hipsters, Fovea Centraleans, Retinal Circus Freaks, Deliriomantics, Mushroom Goddesses, Surfers of the Timewave, Entheogenerators, Brothers and Sisters of the Screaming Abyss, Soluble Fish, Somniloquists, Angels of the Odd, Charioteers of the Gods, Green Men, Neuralchemists, Lexiconjurors, Gothic Wanderers, Mythomantic Mathemystics, Merry Pranksters, Teenage Angsters, Shamans, Boundary Dissolvers, Indigenous Oracles, Paris Peasants, *Enfants Terribles*, Nineteenth-Century Lighthouse Keepers, Calibans, Chaosophers, Hyperboreans, Pre-Raphaelite Succubi, Post-Historical Incubi, Underworld Magicians, Orphic Revellers, Reformed Maldororians, Thelemites, Cosmic Triggers, Philosopher Stoners, Urban Primitives, Residents of Cottage 13, Carvolians, De Selbyites, Voudon Entymologists, Involuntary Mystics, Accidental Transcendentalists, Divine Invaders, Molecular Dervishes, Songsters of the New Erotics, Oneironauts, *Automatistes*, Transmutopians, Dimethyltryptamine Elves, Exphormidable Moose, Somnivores, Loplops, Little Tramps, Salvia Divinorumites, Avalonians, Lemurians, Atlanteans, Sarnians, Fan Men, Linguistic Ontogeneticists, Oulipiens, Blakeans, Etidorhpans, Grail Questers, Nemos, Huxleyan Islanders, Archaic Revivalists, Liberated Androids, Reality Hackers, Neo-Antediluvians, Ayahuasqueros, Curanderos, Saxophonic Pharoahs, Opalescent Infiltrators, Magical Mystery Tourists, Friendly Strangers, Psychidions, Hypnerotomachians, Wollstonecraftians,

Rimbaudelautréamonteans, Letterheads, Deadheads, Godheads, Empty Mirrors, Kama Sutrans, Libertines, Nacreous Lusters, Waking Finnegans, Sleeping Prophets, Exoticians, Sacred Whores, Closet Hermits, Communicating Vessels, Earth Coincidence Control Officers, Sensory Ethnographers, Cloudbusters, Off-Duty Spirit Guides, Qabalistic Fools, Tarot Empresses, Hierophants, Syrinxes, Somnolent Adventurers, Masquerading Sasquatches, Benign Voluptuarians, Lucinellas, Dharma Bums, Vivian Girls, Hanatsu Miroirs, Those Who Ain't the Rosedale Librarians, Animal Communicators, Neurotechnicians, Dark Knights of the Soul, h Tantric Devis, Mantic Devas, Antic Divas, Frantic Devos, Madcap Laughers, Ginnungagappers, Forteans, Crepuscularians, Axolotl Fanciers, Ascended Masters, Ancient Mariners, Cognizens of the Metarealms, Ecstatic Hysterics, Assimilated Wolf Children, Ultima Thuleans, Glossolaliacs, Synaesthetes, Cydonians, Paranoiac Numerologists, Secret Carnival Workers, Cultural Saboteurs, Discordians, Straunge Wunders, Chrysalids, Anna Livia Plurabels, Earwickers, Aurélians, Synchronicitists, Global Village Idiots, Typogres, Synaptic Gliders, Eunoiac Crystallographers, Sleepy Turbines, Midsummer Night Dreamers, Lost Souls, Found Poets, Phantoms of Liberty, Strangers on the Shore, Zygalphiliacs, Loraxes, Quetzalcoatlans, Psychedelic Synthesists, Metal Gurus, Spiral Agitators, North Mutators, Great Canadian Sonneteers, Hunkamoogans, Sonosyntacticians, Ganglian Martyrologists, Cheats of Words, Coma Goats, Prisoners of the Village, Penitent Surreptilians, Watchdogs, Whistleblowers, Wikileakers, Soothspeakers, Outsiders, Black Sheep, White Rabbits, Ugly Ducklings, Beautiful Losers, Steppenwolves, Ice Nymphs, Zequoxes, Xenozaros, Pomps of the Subsoil, Trosperites, Transmorpholutionaries, Oracular Rappers, Noctilucent Ravers, True Hallucinators, Geomancers, Visionary Landscapers, Pantisocrats, Libertatians, Citizens of the Red Night, Zen Detectives, Lapidary Priestesses, Tulpas, Anubises, Xenarthrans, Elevated Water Storage Enthusiasts, Diviners of the *Hockey Ching*, Subgeniuses, Creatures From the Black Lagoon, Leper Messiahs, Bitches Brewers, Van der Graaf Generators, Trout Mask Replicators, Mirror Makers, Thundercats, Riot Grrrls, Mothers of Invention, Sex Pistols, Pawn Hearts, Crazy Diamonds, Osibisans, Piazzollaphiles, Village

Green Preservationists, Practitioners of Cranial Theremin Ouija, Hyperspatial Tour Guides, and Free Thinkers of all Ages, Races, Sexualities, and Creeds!—that I welcome you to the pages of this book, which, quite without realizing it, I began writing thirty-three years ago. That span—representing the golden ratio of my lifetime so far—was preceded by a decade of formative exploration beginning in 1973, when, at age eleven or twelve, I penned an epic called "The Doors of Time." Only one stanza of this opus survives, but as it seems a fitting-enough precursor of what followed, I offer it here for the ages:

> The sediment of life settles on the bottom of your mind
> As the world far beyond recalls the thoughts you left behind
> Like omens of doom
> Your ideas loom
> And open the doors of time

Many lines have since been written (and much sediment settled), but, nearly half a century on, I find myself still close in spirit to that grandiloquent kid who long ago wrung the preceding limerick from the depths of his soul. Should you read on, I hope you will find that there has not been too great a literary decline over the years, and that the poems and stories herein are worth our having sprung open the old doors of time, through which I now invite you to pass.

One other thing. By the time you read this, there may well be a lot going down. For many in the world, there always is. Know that much of what you will be shown is not, technically speaking, real (and that "news" does not equal "truth"). These are days of "Smoking Mirror" (Tezcatlipoca, in Toltec and Aztec lore): a time of much illusion and conflict, of smoke and mirrors. But through this dark looking glass lie adventures beyond our imaginings. We might have to descend from our gleamingly antennaed ivory towers awhile, even as they crumble around us, but there will be new and better, more lucent and inclusive, habitations to build when the dust settles. Meanwhile, shine a light from the highest floor and look out toward the future: a future that, despite the odds—and you'll just have to trust me on this one—will surely be, at least, magnificent.

*SV*

# Part One

## Spiral Agitators and Other Straunge Wunders

"Now a glorious reality!"
—*advertising poster for a forever-unbuilt high-rise tower, seen amid the ruins of a Toronto dairy, circa 1988*

# Transvocations

Robotanists are automated machines that study plants.

Surgeontologists use scalpels to examine the nature of being.

Prostitutors give private lessons to students seeking degrees in copulation.

Anarchitects design houses and other structures for a free and just society according to their own dictates and desires.

Stratagemologists plot wars by cutting precious stones.

Mesmermaids are hypnotically entrancing female servants whose duties are necessarily circumscribed by the fact that they are aquatic, have scales and fins from the waist down, and are believed to be entirely mythical.

Derangers are paid to go berserk in national parks.

Taxidermatologists provide treatments for ailments and cosmetic issues affecting the skin by means of stuffing and preserving the patient. (Not to be mistaken for skin doctors of the same name who conduct their practice in the back seats of cabs.)

Papalaeontologists dig up the bones of prehistoric creatures in order to disprove their existence.

Footballerinas bash heads and tackle one another with orchestral accompaniment in exquisitely choreographed, fiercely competitive dances on stadium AstroTurf.

Accidentists remove your teeth by mistake.

Lexiconjurors tap their wands and pull the words right out of my mouth.

# My Examination

I was next in line but found it increasingly difficult to breathe because they kept hitting me across the chest with long metal shoehorns. Nothing prevented me from striking back except that I knew a confrontation would only prolong my examination. Through the chicken wire I saw three frail beings—men or women, I could not be sure—holding garbage-can lids on which were painted bull's eyes. Each wore earplugs and was dressed in a housecoat made of what appeared to be laminated dog hair, with slippers of the same yellowed material.

When the starting signal flashed, I made my way past the gate onto the dusty track and began my soliloquy as loudly as possible. What I had not expected was that the pigs, which we had earlier injected with amphetamines as part of the test, would stampede toward me as soon as I opened my mouth. Without flubbing a word, however, I pulled out the flares from my leather apron and put the crazed little animals into confusion for a while. This brought some applause from the instructors, but I had the disturbing feeling they were not paying nearly as much attention to the actual words of my speech as they were my reactions to the conditions surrounding it. When I heard a chorus of calculated heckling from behind the chicken wire, along with the interruptive clanging of garbage-can lids, I decided the whole thing was just too much to bear and simply refused to continue. Surrounded as I was by smoke from the flares, I could still make out the sneering faces of my instructors. It was then, Doctor, that I heard that deep, vicious growling at my feet.

# Counting Cars

The government—or perhaps some eccentric individual—had commissioned him to count the cars that passed by a certain roadside statue. The statue was on a slight incline, a lawn otherwise landscaped with only a faux-marble den set into the contour of its slope. At the entrance to the den sat an armchair and a coffee table supporting an old music box in the shape of a schnauzer. When its tail was cranked, the dog emitted a rusty but ennobling interpretation of the national anthem.

Since this quaint station was on my way to work, I agreed, out of a remote sense of admiration, to bring him his breakfast when passing. This consisted of a can of sardines and a loaf of white bread, which he would wash down with expulsions from a water pump. As I'd pause there on the freshly paved surface of the road, he would descend solemnly from his shelter to receive my offering, uttering in exchange a few words for me to ponder while setting about my day.

"They say that if you hold it up to a mirror it will smile at its own reflection, but as soon as you put it down it becomes vicious again," he announced cryptically one morning.

And another time: "Like so many fish upon a trotline, these clouds against the telephone wires."

And his favourite expression: "I have a bird that knows no words."

This last statement was true, for the statue with which he spent his days was of an odd bird, totemic and severe.

In the late afternoon, when returning from work, I'd call out to him as he lay despondently on the shaded marble of his den. But at that hour he would never answer, would seldom even acknowledge me. The chiselled eyes of the winged ornament stared obliquely at the winding asphalt of the road. I could only assume that no cars had passed.

## Ode to Joy

Many years ago, in the middle of the night, I was very sick. As I slept, I dreamt that my stomach pains were being caused by an autoharp embedded in my abdomen. While the autoharp played a most ethereal rendition of "Ode to Joy," an angelic voice sang in such soothing tones that I awoke crying at their beauty.

But the pain was still there and now the lullaby was gone, and even though years have passed I cannot listen to the strains of that melody without clutching my stomach in agony.

So it seems to me that pain can sometimes make us dream of beauty, but that beauty always awakens us to our pain.

# The Grace

We spent that morning in the living room, searching for the previous evening as though it were a dissevered cobra, whose sections were hidden here and there about the room. One piece was found amid a cluster of broken glass, a wine bottle that had shattered near the fractured leg of a coffee table. Another piece was found beneath a pile of scratched-up record albums lying under the stereo, which was covered in yellow and grey feathers of mysterious origin. By turning the now-tattered sofa right-side up, we discovered two more sections of the elusive snake (though they didn't fit together). No matter how diligently we sought, however, we couldn't find the head or the tip of its other extremity, the tail. We still had no idea of the creature's full size, of how much there was still to recover. Even when we checked behind what we all thought to be the object likeliest to conceal a clue—a curiously slashed landscape painting that hung at a disconcerting angle on the fruit-spattered wall—we found nothing but a pair of immaculate formal gloves nailed to the plaster. At another point we became hopeful when someone, crouching in a corner, announced that she'd spotted a few teeth under the shredded pages of an encyclopedia—but they turned out not to be the fangs of a reptile.

When we started to get hungry, and overly frustrated, we decided to take some time out and make breakfast. Stepping into the kitchen, with its lively vegetation overhanging planters on every shelf and sill, and its colourfully wood-stained table and chairs, we felt an immediate sense of relief and, for the moment, forgot about our little hunt. Conversation centred on commonplace topics such as the weather—daylight from a clear sky filled the room—and the general good fortune of our lives at that time, a time considered by all to be simple and pleasant enough. Whatever it was we'd been hoping to divine by the mnemonic sport of our serpentine jigsaw puzzle became an item of greatly reduced significance. In fact, the whole matter of such a reconstruction suddenly seemed comical as we busied ourselves brewing coffee, scrambling eggs, and buttering toast. When the table had been set and we'd taken our places there, it was only half in jest that I offered up a prayer of thanks to whatever deity was behind all this contentment. As if on cue, but without any evident prompt, we joined hands around the table.

All of this may sound a little too suddenly idyllic to anyone unacquainted with the vacillations between distress and euphoria to which the human spirit may be prone. It should be no less surprising, then, that this buoyant atmosphere was soon dissolved, for I was not yet finished saying the grace when a harsh feline snarl interrupted our communion. The two cats—which, until shortly before, had been napping obliviously amid the living-room debris—darted into the kitchen in conflict over an object clenched possessively between the first one's teeth.

Rising from my place at the table, I approached the animals, now hunched near the refrigerator, as they alternately hissed and growled angry threats at one another. Against a hostile resistance, I managed to disengage the cats from their prey. Upon detachment from the object they had so vehemently sought to possess, the two felines scurried from the room as abruptly as they had entered. Now my companions, one by one, rose from their chairs to join me in examining the agent of this commotion.

Lying before us, on the black-and-white-tiled floor, was the hooded neck and cranium of what must have been a very large cobra. Extending from the mouth of this serpent was the end of its own tail, pierced neatly by a venomous fang. We stood silently for a moment in contemplation of this specimen, of its coldly mesmeric quality, and of the all-but-forgotten task renewed by its discovery. With unnecessary caution, I knelt closer and lifted the scaled relic by a fold of its hardened skin. Someone handed me a small, ornate platter from the counter. I placed the object upon it. Then, ignoring our appetites, we slowly left the room and continued our search.

## Possessions

It was heavy—heavier than most birds of its size, though it was not a bird. We kept it in our bureau drawer for a few days but found we were unable to sleep. We put it on our coffee table but this made us nervous, and every time the sunlight struck it the cat would chase its tail with the fervour of a dervish till it threw up on the walls. In time we carted the thing out to the sidewalk and dropped it in the mailbox. All night long, though, the sound of frenzied dogs howling and copulating made us apprehensive and left us feeling edgy for shirking our responsibility. Also, a few purple blotches had begun to show on the skin of our feet and tailbones.

Late that night, on the border of hysteria, we began packing our belongings. As our anxiety mounted, however, we dropped everything and made for the door, leaving cat and possessions behind. But when we reached the outside gate, our exit was blocked by bared canine teeth. At first we cried in terror, beating the ground. Soon we found ourselves imitating the dogs, and that is all I remember.

# What You Need to Know

There is a strong aftertaste of decomposing maple leaves, but it goes away in the second act when the bovine governess upturns a milking stool and exposes her calves. The bannisters are greased, so you must watch yourself on the way up to the washroom, but the treacherous climb, we think you'll agree, is worthwhile, for the view is breathtaking. All the portraits hanging in the west gallery have been commissioned by their subjects, and so certain artistic embellishments, at the sacrifice of realism, are to be expected. Voyeurs are encouraged to use the infrared binoculars provided at no extra charge by the management, although these are not permitted on the third balcony, which overlooks the fabled "Courtyard of Deception." Ambulance service is sporadic in the off-season, so a travellers' course in autosurgery is recommended for the accident-prone. Do not look in cupboards labelled with yellow acetate, and refrain from eating in areas displaying the international symbol for refraining from eating. If you wish to ask a question, raise your hand and wait patiently for a designated respondent to approach. At no time is the biting of fingernails allowed in the presence of Madame Tapir, as this is apt to remind her of her first husband (see local historical brochure entitled *Famous Hunting Accidents and Deaths by Infection*). During the intermission, you may wish to take advantage of the refreshment booth offering free beverages. Be prepared, however, to suffer a few scowls of disapproval from some of the regular patrons, who regard the quenching of thirst as evidence of a weak resolve. Lie down with your cheek to the plush foyer carpeting and lapse into a drooling cataleptic slumber. Don't forget to leave your comments in our guestbook at the end of your stay.

# Scenes from Childhood

In the neighbourhood where I grew up, children exploded frogs with firecrackers, sniffed glue, and stole brassieres from clotheslines. Steaks sizzled on poolside barbecues like ants beneath magnifying glasses.

I still recall the night when humanoid wolves took advantage of my flu-ridden delirium to bugger me as I slept. I went to class the next day, unaware that parental consent was not required for the school nurse to perform bloodletting.

## Jar

Some kids on the sidewalk near a vacant lot have captured something in a glass jar and are ogling it with mischievous delight.

"You better poke some holes in the lid so it can breathe," I suggest as I near them, remembering all the tiny suffocations of my own childhood.

They look at me as if I'm completely mad. Peering closer I see that there's a human tongue inside the jar.

Embarrassed by my absurd suggestion, I continue on my way.

# The Long and the Short of It

The good news is that Jesus has returned.
The bad news is that he's brought his family.
The result is that nothing will ever be the same again (not that
    it ever was).

The good news is that the earth is round (or round*ish*, anyway).
The bad news is that it's floating in space.
The result is that we're going to have to think fast.

The good news is that our bodies are mostly water and so are
    relatively inexpensive to maintain.
The bad news is that, due to global warming, water levels are rising.
The result is that it's impossible to keep your head above water,
    unless you drain it.

The good news is that the century is almost over.
The bad news is that another one is about to begin.
The result is that there is nowhere to hide.

The good news is that free radio waves are passing through us
    at all times.
The bad news is that we can't hear them unless we buy a radio.
The result is that we're left with a sense of violation and dismay
    sometimes unintentionally transmitted to our fellow beings.

The good news is that the government has fallen.
The bad news is that it has fallen on *us*.
The result is that everything will always be the same forever (not
    that it ever wasn't).

The good news is that everything old is new again.
The bad news is that you have to pay for it twice.
The result is that the cyclical is as taxable as the static.

The good news is that the meek shall inherit the earth.
The bad news is that there won't be much left of it after the bold
   have had their day.
The result is that the meek should probably get together and
   attempt to colonize space at their earliest possible convenience.

The good news is that your star is rising.
The bad news is that your power animal is extinct.
The result is that you will more or less break even on the New Age.

The good news is that the Kingdom of Heaven is within.
The bad news is that you can't find the damn thing.
The result is that you will redecorate your apartment.

The good news is that Art is long.
The bad news is that Life is short.
The result is that you should invest in Art while you're still alive.

# Border Dissolution '94

The guy at the customs booth on the American side of the bridge asked us where we lived.

"Turrawno," we chimed proudly.

"What is the purpose of your visit?" he inquired.

"We're just comin' over to shoot a few people, then going right back," I replied.

"Are you bringing over any citrus fruit or pornographic literature?"

"No, sir, we just have some raw beets and a copy of the *Surrealist Manifesto*."

He jutted his crocodilian head a little closer and I halted my reflex to close the window using the automatic button.

"Is that the *First* or *Second* manifesto?" he demanded.

"The *First*," I lied, remembering the ideological rescissions Aragon and Sadoul were forced to make when Communist Party officials objected to aspects of the *Second* manifesto during their visit to Moscow.

This seemed to satisfy our sombre reptilian interrogator, but it was evident he had at least one more good question for us.

"Do either of you have any narcotics or other illicit substances in your possession?"

"No, indeed," asserted my companion.

"Thanks anyway—feeling kinda shitty today," he confided. "Okay, you folks have a nice visit."

"Don't you want to check our trunk?" I offered.

"No, not right now."

At last we were back on our way to the symposium on consciousness and the brain. We weren't really going to shoot anyone, of course, but had felt it best to conceal the true nature of our visit. Even a former president and his wife thought it was okay to have a brain; in fact, they dedicated a whole decade to the thing. But the subject of consciousness, we knew, was another matter entirely.

# An Introduction to Your New TVI Septal Electrode™

Congratulations on choosing Torpor Vigil Industries—the world's finest purveyor of septal electrodes (sales and implantation) since 1691.

The model with which you have been fitted includes a remote control enabling a friend or loved one to transmit euphoriagrams from any location within a three-kilometre radius. There's a synaesthesia adapter for multisensory cross-modal stimulation, as well as an optional audio input that's pitch- and timbre-sensitive. When not in use, this unit produces an automatic 7.83Hz Schumann frequency so you can resonate perpetually with the Earth's ionosphere cavity. Guarantee extends throughout the apocalypse and covers improbable malfunctions due to solar-storm interference (not valid in the event of polar shift or during periods of officially issued Magnetosphere Mutation Warnings).

The TVI Septal Electrode™—a sensible alternative to addictive substances and mundane or immoral entertainments.

# Lucid Dreaming Reality Test

To become adept at lucid dreaming, it is recommended that you perform simple tests intermittently throughout the day as a means of determining that you are really awake. Such exercises, repeated frequently enough, will carry over into your true dreaming state so that the likelihood of becoming conscious of your oneiric condition will be increased.

The following reality checks are provided as examples of this method:

1. Telephone any branch of the Federal Government. If your call is answered, you are probably dreaming. If it is answered by someone other than an alleged government employee—a museum curator, perhaps, or a hair salon receptionist—check the number and dial again.

2. Stare fixedly at the person nearest you, then turn away for a moment. If during this interval the person has transformed into, let's say, a bat-faced magistrate (assuming he or she wasn't already such), you are almost surely asleep.

3. Remove your clothes in a public place and assess the reactions of those around you. Until you have performed this action *while definitely awake*, you will not be able to distinguish between the responses of tangible witnesses and those of dream characters. When in doubt, repeat suggestion #1.

4. Invite a member of the preferred gender to engage in intimate acts with you. If you are dreaming, a glorious realm of sensual fulfillments will be yours to explore (most lucid dreamers describe their somnolent sexual encounters as their most intense and satisfying). If you are not dreaming, you might at least get lucky now and again. Of course, this proposal could have awkward consequences, so it is wise to carry a Lucid Dreamer Reality Test card to present in the event that offence is taken by a corporeal subject of your experimentation.

Note: *Perceived possession of this card does not necessarily mean you are experiencing external reality.*

The practice of these and similar tests of your own invention is sure to provide you with initiation into the fantastical realm of lucid dreaming. Therein you will find the greatest sense of liberation and the truest expression of free will.

Many are they who go through their waking lives unconscious, but few are they with the gift of being conscious while asleep.

## Changeless

I'm in a phone booth. All around me are panthers, jet-black and snarling. The panthers begin to change into Komodo dragons. The ones slow to metamorphose are being eaten by those already transformed. Lava pours down the slope of a nearby volcano. The sun will soon be eclipsed by ash. I don't have a quarter.

# What Happened

Joe was eaten by a tuna.
Marietta was convinced by a spermatozoon.
Clarence was indoctrinated by a curtain.
Sally was bitten by a jack-in-the-box.
Mory was trounced by a gram of saliva.
Tina was capsized by a porcupine.
Salvador was perforated by a weather balloon.
Ursula was basted by a porthole.
Nikolai was reconstituted by a bat.
Grace was hurtled by a steam engine.
Darren was laminated by a milk jug.
Teresa was suctioned by a wheatfield.
Uri was impressed by a squid.
Renée was misplaced by a cloudburst.
Gudbrandur was ploughed by a recipe for marzipan.
Wendy was castrated by a daydream.
Vincent was summoned by a wolf.
Maureen was purged by an ocean liner.
Kamahl was infiltrated by a vestibule.
Lena was deleted by a meadow.
Jim was reimbursed by a falling ocelot.
Astrud was catapulted by a fragrance.
Boris was yanked by a glyptodon.
Doreen was pilfered by a sundial.
Clive was reconfigured by a trampoline.
Indira was courted by a propeller.
Lance was lanced by a lance.
Veronica was crimped by a taxidermal stork.
Jeremy was exorcised by a gearbox.
Serena was orchestrated by a continental shelf.
Guido was pummelled by a kaleidoscope.
Fatima was pursued by a confessional.
Theodore was detonated by a vaccination.
Deborah was lubricated by a chihuahua.
Patrick was inculcated by a rickshaw.

Aurélia was magnified by a rip.
Steven was agitated by a spiral.
Kimberly was ratified by a celery stalk.
Kurt was harpooned by a fire alarm.
Mauve was pigeonholed by a cathedral.
Derek was improved by a moustache.
Sabina was martyred by a snowflake.
Avery was lectured by a goalpost.
Temperance was expunged by a century.
Sebastian was imagined by a girdle.
Jill was stampeded by a sprocket.
Vladimir was mummified by a cricket match.
Tammy was approved by a centipede.

# The Unedited Word of God

*Verily I say unto you: it would be easier for…*

an octopus to smoke a cigar…
a hammerhead shark to win the Kentucky Derby…
a garter snake to drive a cab through the streets of Dublin…
a dwarf hamster to eat the Great Wall of China…
an emu to cook a Spanish omelette…
a pollywog to translate *The Hunting of the Snark* into
    Ojibway…
a Persian cat to have sexual congress with a walrus…
a yellow-bellied sapsucker to conduct Stravinsky's "Octet
    for Wind Instruments"…
a mongoose to deal blackjack…
a ruby-throated hummingbird to unscrew the lid of a
    ketchup bottle…
a wombat to jump the Grand Canyon on a tricycle…
a praying mantis to milk a cow…
a rhinoceros to do a jigsaw puzzle of the Taj Mahal…
a fruit fly to laugh…
a tarantula to operate a jackhammer in the middle of a
    blizzard…
a flying fish to synthesize mescaline…
a butterfly flapping its wings in Peru to cause a tornado
    in China…
an Egyptian tortoise to hit a hole-in-one on a par-4 dogleg…
a wolverine to assassinate the pope using a slingshot loaded
    with overcooked lima beans…
a warthog to put a condom on a blue whale…
a red snapper, or anything for that matter, to mix a proper
    martini…
an anaconda to play the part of Malvolio in *Twelfth Night*
    before an audience of Shakespeare scholars…

a Western screech owl to throw a javelin through the hole of
    a doughnut at a distance equivalent to the length of three
    soccer fields...
a nightingale to sire a cactus...
a badger to fart a hurricane...
a team of golden lion tamarin monkeys to defeat the
    defending Stanley Cup champions on home ice...
a tarsier to lasso a cruise missile with a vermicelli noodle...
a honey possum to sculpt a perfect likeness of Aleister Crowley
    out of marmalade and motor oil...
a manatee to dance the tango on a serving spoon...
a camel to pass through the eye of a needle...

*than for a rich man to enter the Kingdom of Heaven.*

# The Last Invitation of Summer

Dear Madam Quince-Dowry,

As summer is ending I felt it incumbent on me to invite you to a thunderstorm that is scheduled to take place outside the herring factory this evening at dusk. You needn't dress in any but the most perfunctory manner nor bring any crickets (there will be plenty of those!) as I myself will be wearing but a thin military camisole from the pelvic region upward and will be toting a gecko or two. By the way, I can see the dunes from the third-storey window of my cabin, and they are absolutely still—not a grain moving. I know not what lies within them, but I have a friend (a recent lover of yours, say the boys down at the pub) who is a spelunker and *he* says he's not interested in them because they're not caves. I've asked him not to accompany us and he's more than happy to oblige. Will there be fireworks? No, there will not be fireworks, but there's a young Christian girl (a bastard daughter of yours, if the Reverend Glitch is to be believed) who will read from the Bible for tips and cheese. I'm so excited by the prospect that you might actually join me on this little outing that I've quite been masturbating—and furiously!—all morning in anticipation. Dr. Craque (the same fellow who, according to the papers, performed your last hysterectomy) told me this would be good for calming my nerves—indeed the opposite, for I find myself in a neuromanic frenzy just contemplating the notion that you and I might picnic together this very evening beneath those same bolts of lightning that are sure to set the Riddley barns aflame again. Have you any toothpaste? Be sure to screw the cap on tightly: I have an aunt (one of your mothers, I believe?) who died not long ago from leaving the cap unscrewed on a tube of Sterident. The poor woman left the world without a will, and we've been squabbling over her miniature teacups ever since. Please respond by flare (red yes, blue no) as soon as possible. I must close now as my wife (your squirrel-catcher in a past life, swears Sturluson, the trance medium and elbow boxer) is leaving on her errands and I would like her to deliver this letter, along with the rooster I borrowed, to your hallowed door.

With fondest regards to you and your lovely poodle (does she suffer yet?),

Your dithering suitor,

Andromimicus "Andy" Clump, Esq.

## Malpractice

Three aspirins and an enema to cure a woman in the throes of labour.

Electroshock therapy to treat a young girl suffering from tonsillitis.

Removal of the gallbladder to heal an elderly male frostbite victim.

A plaster cast over the left forearm and wrist to restore the memory of a middle-aged female amnesiac.

Circumcision to alleviate the symptoms of a persistent head cold afflicting a teenage boy.

# The Deregulation of Nature

*Nature is being deregulated. Who is going to run the Animal Kingdom now?*

God is not dead—He's just encountered a little financial difficulty. What does this mean to you? Well, first of all it means that certain systems and services once the exclusive domain of the Almighty are now up for grabs: Nature is no longer a monopoly. Starting with some wildlife maintenance strategies and atmospheric conditions, natural phenomena will be in the hands of Free Enterprise. It's up to companies such as Torpor Vigil Industries to assume responsibility for these operations, and ensure that the natural world is run with the same integrity, reliability, and creativity you've come to expect from the Man Upstairs.

Can TVI uphold the same standard of excellence established by the Creator? The answer is *yes*—in fact, we believe there's room for improvement. Already we've made some advances in this direction. During the early stages of deregulation, our company was the first to introduce zebra mussels into freshwater Canadian rivers and bays. Those waters are now cleaner than they've been in ages, and the mussels are flourishing in their new environments. And that's just a hint of the developments we have in store.

For example, you've probably been hearing a lot lately about the migratory falterings of various creatures of air and sea. In the face of instinct cutbacks these species are becoming confused, and often fail to successfully navigate the age-old patterns their ancestors so deftly and intuitively executed. At TVI we've tabled a plan to incrementally raise the instinct awareness levels in afflicted fish, birds, and insects. With TVI restoring innate migratory aptitudes, you can rest assured that a flock of monarch butterflies destined for the Transvolcanic Plateau in Mexico will not end up at a truck stop in Langenburg, Saskatchewan.

And who hasn't seen news reports about infertile tortoises, hermaphroditic birds, and six-eyed fish? Perhaps you've even caught one of the latter yourself, while casting your line at the cottage. True, for the most part, these abnormalities are side effects of chemical dumping, nuclear testing, and other human activities—but humans are a part of Nature, and other species must be equipped to adapt to the novelties introduced by *Homo sapiens*. Mutational Versatility has always been a major part of TVI's mandate. We're thrilled to have the opportunity to put our specialized techniques in the service of our Gaian siblings—to accelerate the evolutionary adaptability toward which all sensible species strive.

Also on the agenda is the expansion of our role as chemical supplier to meet the pharmacological needs of various insects, arachnids, and cephalopods: bombardier beetles need hydroquinone to stun their assailants, spiders need vortexylene to spin their webs, cuttlefish need customized ink to…well, we're not entirely sure—but where there's a need for chemistry in the Wild Kingdom, our laboratories will be ready with the goods.

And this brings us to what may well be the most exciting aspect of our new endeavours: Cyclonic Generation and Deployment. I'm sure you'll agree that there's nothing quite so thrilling and beautiful as a good tornado. But if you happen to be living in the path of one of these pneumatic wonders, it may be difficult to fully enjoy its poetic grandeur. All in all, tornadoes have been dispensed too randomly. The haphazard, "anything goes" approach to cyclone vending just does not work in our modern industrialized civilization.

The answer? Tornado Vigilance Induction—a computer-engineered system for the controlled instigation and direction of tornadoes. Provinces and states that choose membership in our TVI program will be guaranteed, for a seasonal fee, that tornadoes strike only in designated geographical areas at preordained times. Not only will this eliminate the danger and expense of unwanted cyclones, it will open the door to entrepreneurial and recreational opportunities unimaginable prior to deregulation. Tornado watching, in designated "twister valleys," will become the spectator sport par excellence. The potential tourism and broadcast revenue this represents for subscribing governments is stupendous. Furthermore, thrill-seeker pastimes such as skydiving, bungee jumping, and golfing will be all but forgotten in the wake of the tornado-surfing craze that's sure to sweep the continent. Why be the daredevil who dangles from a cliff or hurtles down the Falls in a barrel—or, for that matter, the couch salamander who watches it all on TV—when you can safely spiral through the air in a specially designed Torsurfer™ suit from TVI?

The possibilities, as you can surely begin to imagine, are endless. Not since the Garden of Eden has humanity been granted so magnificent an opportunity to benignly direct the natural domain. This time we won't blow it. With Torpor Vigil Industries leading the way, the future of our earthly adventure will be one of efficiency, fascination, and corporate good sense.

While God's off playing dice with the Universe, we'll be down here taking care of business—the biggest business of all, that is: Nature.

# Sentence

1. This sentence uses only recycled words.

2. Using this sentence for any purpose other than communication or information storage may be dangerous.

3. This sentence began life as an artifact.

4. This sentence has a fixed meaning that does not change, whether spoken in a catacomb or spoken in a control tower.

5. This sentence may be used repeatedly without deterioration, though overuse may lead to apparent diminishment of its significance (and in extreme cases insanity or the delusion of enlightenment).

6. This sentence may be spoken with the impunity of ignorance by animals, or computers, capable of mimicking human speech.

7. This sentence is not immune to polyglot shift: if it has been written, spoken, or otherwise processed in any language other than English, a translation has occurred; in this event, please contact the manufacturer should you wish to be issued the original English-language version.

8. This sentence should not be taken literally by pregnant women, or laterally by dyslexics.

9. This sentence may be used to rouse someone from a deep slumber if spoken loudly enough (optimal volume will vary according to proximity of speaker to subject, and density of the sleep state).

10. This sentence is communicable and may be transmitted orally, or in Braille, through photic projection and similar forms of reproduction, via the print medium, telepathically, or by means not yet imagined.

11. This sentence can be stared at without comprehension.

12. This sentence is several anagrams.

# The Serpentine Dance*

The cheery voyeur's queer game
Detonates the seaborne corpse,
A vacillating coma edifies
The Peruvian marauder!

Spurred to cavalier profundity
The actress oozes perfumes,
Odoriferous vagabond of the mire
Awaiting the blaze of flyweight brains.

This scummy aeon never quits snivelling,
Weighing events like dough and mutton,
A moaning ape reweaves its apparel
Like a poor Chilean nun with tanned loins.

Taoist eyes reveal the ripening of new sex,
Dazed with the amorous knowledge of death,
Bogus Malayan cygnets dozing like seaway freighters
Evoking laughter's fire.

Veering at the mercy of decadent thighs,
In billowing abandonment,
A serpent dancing on the coy derrière,
A baton in the bawdy dunes.

Sobbing and laughing from the fjord to the poorhouse,
The tattooed infant teethes,
Balancing maliciously over the sea
In the jejune elephantine dawn.

Punks swallow tons of carp and sigh in awe,
Their voices chime with fins,
Quiet railways plunge into the boiling surf
Where lowly virgins sway in dinghies.

A chemical fountain floods the parlour of grace,
The grand dance of desolate glaciers
Which lay chained to remote beaches
Where birds and rodents thaw.

Crazed Bohemian jets buried in vines
And amber vapour,
A quiet ceiling of paraseminal liquid
Covers the stars!

* a quasileximatic translation of Baudelaire's "Le serpent qui danse"

# The Black Domain

First slide, please.

1. Here we see the Forest of Blackness itself. I would say the entrance to the forest, but it has no entrance: you're either in it or not. But this is the point at which, on my fifth visit, I became "inside" the forest. And I call it a forest, though much of what constitutes this zone is evidently synthetic, rather than organic. For that matter, it's not strictly black, either. The tonal range in most areas is pretty limited, though—say, from charcoal to jet black. I used a flash for this shot, but in upcoming slides you'll get a better idea of the ghostly surface radiance I mentioned earlier. Note the sequoia-like trunks encoiled by smooth rubber tubes. The ground looks like granite, doesn't it, but it was actually spongy underfoot. Now, what startles me in this photo is the owl. When you look at this image, it's the first thing your eyes are drawn to: this brooding sentinel glaring down at the camera lens. I had no idea it was there at the time. It didn't make a sound. Mind you, nothing makes a sound in that hermetic landscape. I couldn't even hear my own tinnitus. Next slide, please.

2. The same, but without the flash. No owl this time. You can see where it was—that area without detail. Some surfaces seem to emit light—blackly translucent auras. The slightly granular look of this scene is the result of the film speed I used. Even a high-resolution film, however, would have failed to convey the hyperlucid quality of the zone. On to the next slide…

3. Yes—your fashionable narrator. I used a tripod and flash for this. I wanted to show that materials exotic to the forest maintain their chromatic integrity within its bounds—hence, my lime-green suspenders and orange shirt. Not exactly standard attire for a sober researcher such as myself, but… All right, another slide— No, could you just go back to the last one for a moment, please?

Do you see that—in the lower left of the frame? Yes, it is a football. A perfectly natural—well, not natural, but a real football.

I picked it up: it was typical in every way—size, weight, feel, even scent—of a brand-new cowhide football, except it was utterly black and there was no label on it. I put it in my camera bag, but it was gone when I returned: one of several objects I've tried without success to bring back from the forest. I'd love to have even one of them to pass around to you. Uh…I'll answer questions after the slides, if you don't mind waiting. Okay—slide, please.

4. Yes. This is not a mistake. It's a picture of one of the areas of the zone that is so black… Well, you can see what I mean: no surface reflection at all. And this was taken with the flash. Took me ages to get through this part because I just inched my way along, afraid I might land in a pit or tumble from a cliff, but fortunately… Well, I think it's fortunate, anyway. Slide number five, please.

5. Here we are on the other side of that particular voidlike area. This shows you how voluptuous the forest can be. Moss-covered knolls and lustrous rocks…weeping willows and enormous ferns. What appear to be giant glass eggs… Don't know what they are. They have marvellously articulated patterns just beneath their translucent contours: arabesque swirls like turbulence renderings, intricate mazelike lines, tracery reminiscent of ocean-current maps, all displayed in a lavish variety of ebony gradations. Yes, blackness is relative: even white I now look upon as merely a shade of black. Next image, if you would.

6. We're getting deeper into the forest now. And I say "deeper" but I mean it only with regard to this particular excursion. Notice the jagged vertical slabs of what looks like obsidian mirror. It doesn't photograph well, but up close each of these slabs appears to be a window onto a different area of the forest. The views presented—three-dimensional, as if holographic—are negatives; that is, what would be the darkest tones appear as the lightest. Very subtle—it took me a while to figure out what was different about these "vistas," but I think that's it. They're reversal windows affording

remote views...sort of virtual small-scale dioramas projecting other regions of the Forest of Blackness. Occasionally these slabs are grouped in configurations reminiscent of prehistoric stone circles. They tend to appear in areas where black grass forms the dominant ground cover.

I didn't encounter any this trip, but there are a lot of snakes in the forest. They seem to be—apart from moths, which I'll get to later—the only animate creatures native to the zone. (There's one other known exception, come to think of it—and rather a dramatic one—but I'll come to that in time.) These snakes are exceptionally thin, and either extremely swift or completely motionless. One of my strangest forest experiences was coming across a huge mating ball of such serpents. One moment it would be writhing wildly; the next, utterly still, like an overgrowth of vines or roots. The snakes are eyed, but without mouths. Most are of a uniform blackness, with no sign of scales. On some, I've observed herringbone patterns along the back. Others are marked by parallel circular bands. One had a meandering line of a relatively light shade running from the base of its head to the tip of its tail. My presence, by the way, had no evident effect upon their activity.

Now, I've mentioned the animate creatures as a prelude to this next slide, which features one of the inanimate creatures. You can run the next slide now.

7. Startling, isn't it? This close-up of the dog's head was taken without a flash. The exposure time was at least ten seconds, yet there's no blurring except in the eyes. It's quite haunting. From what I've seen, these dogs are always motionless, statuesque—apart from the eyes, which peer at you as you approach. They seem to be retrievers, though I haven't managed to match them with any known breed. Pet them, they feel like dogs, but they're not breathing. I don't know what they're doing. It's...poignant, somehow. I love those dogs. Would you click us on to the next frame, please?

8. Here he is again, the poor chap. Seems content enough, but those eyes! All right, on to number—let's see—number nine, please. Thank you.

9. What this is, it's... I'm behind a waterfall. I'm looking out from a sort of grotto, photographing this tattered sheet of black water as it cascades over the jutting rocks above. Its soundless flow was mesmerizing, but after a time I began to feel more and more spooked by the mysterious pitch darkness of the cavern behind me. The hollow silence of the forest can be unsettling at times. Next slide...

10. The environs of the waterfall, seen from an approach of several metres. I backtracked to get this photo—or did I get the slides reversed? Both, come to think of it. The water gives the impression of a shimmering, darkly luminous drapery. The vegetation is also somewhat hazy—the leaves are, anyway—because of the long exposure and because of a gentle rustling that I attribute to the effect of a wind. Not a typical wind. Neither my hair nor my clothing was stirred by it. I call this phenomenon the "parazephyr": a subtle current not reliant upon air molecules for its material influence. And while I couldn't detect it as a physical force, I did have a kind of internal awareness of its presence—somewhat like the mild exhilaration many of us are prone to at the approach of an electrical storm.

The temperature of the zone is approximately 23°C. Nevertheless, an eclectic polyclimatic assortment of plant life flourishes there. Tropical ferns and vines—that appears to be *Banisteriopsis caapi* in the foreground—thrive alongside peyote and other forms of cactus, while mushrooms such as *Stropharia cubensis* spring up alongside the trunks of sumac, silver (if it can still be called silver) maple, and other typically northern species of tree. I tasted the sap of one such maple, but it was completely flavourless. It occurred to me that my sense of taste might be nullified in that setting, but when I put my finger to my lips after pricking it on a cactus needle I could taste the blood. Later, when I bit into a dusky peach I couldn't taste it at all, though the aroma of this otherworldly fruit was magnificent.

I'd like to stay on this slide just a bit longer. Some of the more intriguing things in this scene are less easy to pick out. For example, that cone-shaped object between those two irises—it's partly concealed by a thistle... Do you see what I'm talking about now? It's hard to tell what it is from this photo—I've got a much better shot of the thing, but it's at my publisher's right now. If that thistle wasn't in the way, I'm sure you'd all recognize it as being a component of every standard household washing machine. The name of the thing has slipped my mind—it's that plastic spindle that swooshes the clothes around. And if any one of you can tell me why there should be such a contrivance sitting in the middle of an uninhabited forest, I'll do your laundry for a month. I guess it's kind of like that football—an incongruous artifact designed to spin and cause a lot of commotion.

Okay—what else do we have here? You see that small cedar tree on the right? It's fake—plastic. And those rocks on the far left? More dogs, from the rear this time. One's sprawled over the back of the other, which is curled up on the forest floor. The muzzle of a third can just be seen poking up over the haunch of the sprawler. A small pile of dogs. They're probably still stacked there. So let's let sleeping dogs lie… Sorry, I couldn't resist. I think it's time for another slide.

11. This slide reveals the terrain just beyond the luxuriantly wooded area pictured in the preceding shot: a jet-black lawn stretching as far as the eye could see, which was about forty or fifty metres before the setting became indistinct. The grass blades were ankle-deep—a lush ebony carpet covering the flat expanse of a seemingly phosphorescent field. The overall effect, poorly conveyed by this photo, was of a country field on a moonlit night. But there was no moon and there was no sky. The murky radiance seemed to emanate from the lawn itself. Moreover, my physical presence appeared to change the surrounding landscape such that the ground within about a three-metre radius of my body was brighter than the outlying area. Whatever force was at play also caused my footprints to remain noticeably luminous for some distance behind me as I continued to explore the region.

12. The next slide…yes—thank you…shows part of this brilliant trail I've forged. This was certainly the quietest stroll in the country I've ever taken. Remember that this realm is silent. You can see it and feel it and sometimes smell it; but you can't taste it or hear it. And the only souvenirs I've managed to smuggle across the border—intangible as it is—are these images. Next slide.

13. This is a very long exposure, taken after several minutes of walking across this broad plateau. I said several minutes, but, as on previous visits, my watch had stopped when I entered the forest. Invariably, upon once again finding myself no longer within this black region, I discover that not more than six or seven minutes of actual time has elapsed. As for direction, I've twice brought a compass to the forest and both times the needle has spun continuously, as if at the centre of a magnetic vortex. Technologically, the only instrument that has behaved itself in this landscape is the camera. Then again, I haven't performed much by way of experimentation. I'll have to bring a cellphone next time. If any of you get a call and there's silence on the other end, take note—it might be me ringing you from within the Forest of Blackness.

And, as I mentioned, the term *forest* is a misnomer. Obviously the place is geologically more eclectic than a mere woodland. Now that this zone has revealed a greater range of its constitution than what I glimpsed on my initial visit, I should probably rename it. Perhaps calling it the Black Domain, for example, would be more appropriate. Who knows—I might one day discover a city there. With any luck, it will have a better public transit system than the one you have here. I've got to blame my late arrival on something.

Okay, back to the lawn. There's a circular glow in the distance, more pronounced than it had appeared to me because I left the camera shutter open for about a dozen seconds. I didn't know what it was at the time. It's… Well, let's move on to the next slide.

14. Here's a… Here's an upside-down slide. Can you…? Thank you, projectionist. Here's a cliff face, smooth and globular, like melted wax. This is huge, stretching upward and to both sides as far as I could see. It disappears in total blackness about fifteen metres up. That glow that was visible from a distance is the entrance to a cavern. Why some caverns are illuminated and others dark, I couldn't tell you. My eyes had become accustomed to the sub-gloamy conditions, so this tunnel mouth seemed relatively brilliant. Rather than following the vertical cliff face to right or left, I decided to explore the cave. If you could click us forward a frame…

15. I've used a flash to highlight the mottled surface features of the passageway, which is approximately two-and-a-half metres wide and just as tall. Its surface is covered in splotchy lichen, lending the interior an ambience of inviting softness. The grass has given way to a puttylike humus, which in turn is succeeded, as we move through the tunnel... Next slide, please...

16. ...by fine-grained sand. The slope's descent becomes steeper at this point, and the sand denser. I paused here to remove my hiking shoes and socks, partly to facilitate ingress and partly, well, because I felt like it. Note the vermiform depressions in the black sand. These patterns I found oddly alluring, as if they were a welcoming calligraphy to which I unconsciously responded. Rarely have I felt so at home in an environment, though customarily I'm drawn to a more colourful decor. Another slide, if you don't mind. Thank you.

17. And we've arrived. What strange splendour: the interior of my moth grotto, as I call it. Such an extraordinary, lovely, pacific chamber—yet not without its ominous aspects, which my rambling commentary will detail.

This is the first wide-angle shot of the cave. The tripod was set on the threshold, just before the tiered descent to the sand floor. The contours of the curved walls and ceiling gave me a sense of being within an enormous black eggshell. And while the initial impression of this ovoid hollow is of absolute smoothness, closer inspection— and you'll see this when we get to the next slide—reveals a delicate embossing to the entire surface, a voluptuous textural marbling, like an elaborate non-repetitive Art Nouveau pattern infecting every inch of the osseous interior.

This glorious embellishment is mirrored in the glasslike surface of the pool. Even the sand surrounding the pool is scalloped in swirling ridges, as if carved to replicate the grain of an exquisite wood. The only part of the decor that contrasts with this hallucinatory motif is seen on the far expanse, more or less opposite the entranceway. This is the carpet of moths, but I'll discuss that when we examine it from a closer vantage. Another slide, please.

18. This is a timed-release photo from the same position. The foreground, including your guide, is flash-lit. After the initial shot, I'd wandered down into the chamber to explore its wonders. My enthrallment was unrestrained, as you can see from my expression. Never before had I encountered a setting that inspired such euphoria and provided such aesthetic satisfaction. By this stage of my journey, I had been within the zone longer than in any of my previous incursions. I was feeling more and more remote from the ordinary world—remote, yet intensely comfortable, as though I'd stumbled upon a space that was the topological analogue of my own soul. When I say that now, it sounds arrogant because this room was exceptionally beautiful. Yet, at the time, there was a tremendous sense of rightness to my being there. And I don't know quite how I've been changed, but I still carry this conviction that entering the moth grotto was a metamorphic experience.

Well, enough mystical testimony for now. On with the objective inspection of the cave. This next slide…that's the one…

19. …is a close-up of an arm's-length patch of wall design. I almost said "wallpaper." Believe me, if I could replicate this pattern on paper, it would cover the walls of my own abode. It's a natural, perhaps supernatural, intaglio carved upon an even more complex chaos of lines in various gradations of black. My first thought was that this opulent lineation was a language, but one my species was not cognitively equipped to comprehend. As I stared into this profusion of lines, I became awed by a compelling notion, a forceful intimation: this pattern was not a language, at least not merely a language, but an organism itself—an intelligence that had *spoken itself* onto the surface of this ovarian catacomb. And the longer I stared, the more profound the revelation. The mesmeric weave pounced out at me, through me, in a holographic explosion. The pattern—now envelopingly three-dimensional—was no longer articulated by shades of black. It was alive with every conceivable colour, saturated beyond imagination with otherworldly hues, a sublime prismatic flood of kaleidoscopic variegation, ever shifting, ever… I was just demolished by its beauty. Totally transfixed, I submitted almost painfully to this rapture of tonality and form.

How long this communion lasted, how long I was in its throes, I've no way of telling. When I finally turned my head I saw that the whole cavern was infused with the same magnificence, a living cathedral of supernovan glory. But almost instantly, upon my turning, the spectacle disappeared, as if sucked back into the walls and drained of colour.

Dazzled to the point of vertigo, I dropped to my knees and convalesced in this supplicant position, pondering what the hell had happened. Did I somehow trigger this psychedelic refulgence by neurally interfacing with the sector of the pattern upon which I gazed? Or was it all internal? Did I attain a type of spontaneous samadhi by concentrating on some sort of hyper-fresco—an abstract, perhaps alien, motif latent with vision-inducing dynamism? Whatever it was that happened, and however it happened, it happened only once. I may have become too cerebrally agitated, or maybe I achieved "tolerance"—but further meditation upon the pattern failed to activate the spectacle. Regardless, the walls did yield some interesting impressions as I resumed my scrutiny of the interior.

Now, if our projectionist is still awake after all that, we'll have the next slide. Thank you.

20. Further along the elliptical wall... Similar to the last patch, but from closer range. I used a close-up lens to zone in on an area about the size of a...I don't know, a laptop computer screen. The detail seems to be infinite, reducing almost fractally to a microscopic degree. There was no recurrence of colour or animation, but whenever I gazed steadily and directly at the pattern, images unfurled before my eyes—like a morphing tapestry of unconscious generation. I'll spare you the particulars of what I saw, but I'm convinced by the personal nature of this picture play that what is seen is dependent upon the psyche of the observer. The ovarian wall, in this regard, is a metaphysical mirror. I've named this endless pattern the Vision Engine—but that doesn't adequately convey its insistently vital quality. Maybe we should call it the *Living* Vision Engine: let's see, what would that be...the "LiViEn," for short. Wish I'd thought of that before going to press. Slide number, uh, twenty-one, please.

21. Proceeding in a counterclockwise manner, we come to the narrower end of the egg-shaped cave, the end furthest from the entrance. I've employed a diffused flash and a long exposure to capture this wide-angle impression of the curving end wall and part of the ceiling. The tripod was planted at the sandy bank of the pool. I invite you to stare at the middle of the screen, to focus unwaveringly on any point of the pattern's multi-latticed skein. If you can perform this exercise steadily for a minute or so, you may find that your focal area expands to take in the periphery. This simple method of optical concentration—referred to as "visual flooding" by the writer Christopher Dewdney—is what I practised when viewing the cavern walls. When it works, especially when applied to a densely filigreed visual plane, this technique opens (to quote another visionary author) "the doors of perception."

If you're not "seeing things"—and it sounds like a few of you already are—you may want to try again later. I'll be passing around some large-format prints featuring sections of the LiViEn prior to the question period.

We're going to move on now, in our counterclockwise tour, so that I can introduce you to the moths. I hate to interrupt anyone's trance...but I'm eager to show you this next slide.

22. Ah, terrific—you're picking up on my projection cues very well. Soon I won't need to prompt you at all—we'll just do this telepathically.

Okay—here it is: the mosaic of moths. About a third of it, anyway—as much as I could fit in the frame using a standard lens while standing on the bank of the pool. There's only about two metres from the pool to the moth wall, which, as you can probably tell, is considerably flatter than the other portions of the shell. The camera was hand-held and the aperture was rather too large, given the charge of the flash—hence the overexposure responsible for the ethereal quality of this shot, which I quite like. I think the next image is the close-up: it will give you a better impression of the moths—from a lepidopterous if not an æsthetic viewpoint. So...

23. Yes, this is the close-up. I'll try to skip the technical details from here on—those of you who are photographers are welcome to

interrogate me later. I'll say only that this is the most successful of several close-ups I took. It shows the moths in suspended animation—their collective fluttering produced hypnotic undulations—and it reveals the fine, subtle tracery each possessed, apparently in mimicry of the ambient ornamentation.

These moths—look how closely gathered they are, not a speck of wall visible—resemble species of the noctuid family, though they're distinct enough to be unclassifiable. The markings alone make them unique, but also the head is anomalously large by comparison to the body. My presence didn't distract them at all—even when I brushed them lightly with my fingertips, they merely adjusted their position and continued clinging to the wall. A fragrance reminiscent of hyacinths, but muskier, emanated from this soft quivering drapery of moths.

For the next picture, I switched to a wide-angle lens and set up my tripod at the edge of the pool... Next, please...

24. And this is the result: a seamless cloak of moths that covers an area, extending beyond the frame, possibly equal to the surface of the pool. I felt oddly privileged to behold this black wingscape. Choreographies of fluttering would erupt in swirls. The vibratory clusters sometimes collided or converged in spellbinding arabesques. An exhilarating entrancement overcame me as I watched the textural oscillations of this living carpet. If I ever manage to return to the Forest of Blackness, I hope I have a video camera with me. Now for the pool. Slide twenty-five, please.

25. This slide is actually out of sequence. I'd intended to photograph the pool more methodically after documenting the moth wall, but I didn't get the chance. So what you're seeing is basically a snapshot taken shortly after stepping into the cavern. The black gleaming surface, reflecting the dome of the chamber, is devoid of even the merest ripple. It remained so, remarkably, when I entered the pool.

Being in this wondrous setting called for a baptism of sorts. I wasn't even sure the stuff was water: jet-black like printers' ink, but it seemed like water when I put my hand in. Except that it would not ripple. My fingers moved through this liquid as they would through water, and when I withdrew my hand there was a dampness to my skin. But I couldn't make a splash, or even the slightest billow. As foolish as it seems in retrospect, I was determined to enter the pool.

Leaving my clothes on the sandy bank, I lowered myself over the edge, which was almost level with the surface of the water. Probing with my legs, I discovered that the pool extended horizontally beneath the shelf of rock on which I'd been standing. Maybe it was really part of a lake, or even an ocean, the greater shores of which lay beyond the territory of my present adventure. (If such was the case, might I at the outset of some future visit find myself teleported to the middle of a vast sea of blackness?) All I could feel was water—no way of judging its depth. Euphorically, I pushed off from the bank and floated on my back to the centre of the pool, just far enough that my feet could not touch the ledge.

From this strange well, I gazed up at the gloriously reticulated dome of the moth grotto. An ecstatic surge of energy charged every cell of my body with its expansive revelatory force. I was immersed in a power spot. The boundaries of my physical self— Well, I'll spare you another lapse into quasi-religious reportage. I lost awareness of my physical self, yet was still conscious of the need to breathe in order to stay afloat, not to mention stay alive. But no volition was required: my nervous system knew what was expected of it and got along perfectly well without me, so to speak.

When this spell began to lift and I again felt my body treading the amniotic blackness, I yielded to the temptation of total submersion. I just wanted to dunk myself completely once before leaving this preternatural isolation tank. Closing my eyes and sealing my nostrils between finger and thumb, I took a big gulp of air and plunged vertically, using my free arm to propel me deeper into the pool. Still in downward motion, I felt a large, slick, blubbery form slide across my left thigh. Before I could do a proper job of panicking—frozen with terror was as far as I got—my lower legs were encoiled by tentacles of a similar flaccid, rubbery constitution. There was nothing ostensibly threatening about the way this creature, assuming there was only one, greeted me; nevertheless—warm welcome or not—it wasn't the time for interspecies diplomacy. My previous tranquil complacency had been displaced so rapidly by a state of sheer horror, I was in danger of expelling the air from my lungs.

With a couple of kicks, my legs slipped from the serpentine embrace and I shot toward the surface. Gasping and flailing—my limbs felt like soggy cardboard—I floundered to the ledge of land from which I'd entered the pool. My efforts to raise myself onto the shore must've been quite comical, but I was still seized by fear of being ensnared or devoured by one of the mysterious forms lurking below. No siren song, however alluring, could have enticed me to return to the pool once I was back on dry land.

And speaking of sound, as soon as I emerged from the water I became aware of a low murmuring drone. As I looked about me to determine the source of this ethereal tone, I could hear also the panting of my own breath. Then a new noise, growing swiftly in volume, caused me to look again at the opaque surface of the pool. Waves were forming on its previously flat surface, rolling concentrically till they lapped at the shore. A vortex began to occur in the middle of the pool, and soon a counterclockwise swirl chiselled the water into a turbulent spiral. My ears, unaccustomed to sound, were filled with the reverberative roar of the whirlpool, as if it were an ocean maelstrom. Stricken by a rush of vertigo, I stepped back from the edge, shivering now as the sheen of liquid started to evaporate from my skin. A moth landed on my wrist, then another on my neck, and several more on my spine and shoulders. I turned to see the entire mosaic crumbling tile by tile as the moths fluttered from the wall to adorn my body. The after-effects of my underwater trauma dissolved in a giddy scintillation that rose tremulously from the tip of my spine to the top of my skull. I was now almost entirely covered in a quivering noctuid cloak. The oddly sensuous taction of myriad insect legs upon my flesh made me feel at once placid and unbearably skittish. This vibration of thousands of tiny wings—that was the origin of the drone I'd heard upon resurfacing. And now the drone was within me as well, fluxing discordantly with the vorticular resonance of the pool.

The slide you are about to see is a self-portrait taken by a man utterly enmothed. Slide, please.

26. Yes—it is astounding, isn't it? Fortuitously, after photographing the moth wall, I'd left the camera on the tripod, its settings unaltered. I could see only by fluttering my eyelids and shaking my head to disengage the moths clustered on my face. One finger was all I needed to set the timing mechanism and trigger the shutter. I ambled backwards, careful not to harm the living garment that both enwrapped and enraptured me. With uplifted arms, I became the strange statue you observe on the screen. Notice that beyond me, the wall that had been occupied by the moths is absolutely black, is not even a wall.

This image of me cocooned in the moth grotto is the last from within the region of blackness. Though I have attempted to re-enter the zone many times since, by readying myself mentally and gesturally, as described in my preamble to this lecture, all efforts have been in vain—perhaps because the effort itself, too conscientiously applied, precluded my admission. Or perhaps I have already reached the limit of what can be revealed to me, of what I am disposed to sustain in such a realm.

There is one more frame of film I exposed in this sequence. Moments after the camera captured my moth-embellished pose, I rigged the device for another shot. My breathing was hindered more and more by the overlay of wings. There was little hope now of clearing my eyelids without harming the delicate creatures that roosted there. Sightless and covered in moths, like a somnambulant entomologist overcome by his specimens, I groped my way toward the camera. Only with difficulty did I perform the necessary prehensile gestures to set the timer in motion. Retreating softly into focus range, barely breathing, I awaited the click of the shutter. In that interval, those few mechanical seconds between action and reaction, I left the Black Domain. I am standing in my living room, clothed as I was upon entering the forest, my eyes closed as if in prayer.

Last slide, please.

61

# Part Two

## Floors of Enduring Beauty and Other Fine Quality Realities

"Oft in my waking dreams do I
Live o'er again that happy hour
When midway on the mount I lay
Beside the ruined tower"
—*Samuel Taylor Coleridge*

# Transvocations Two

Texterminators are hired to eliminate undesirable and potentially virulent writings.

Atrocity planners provide practical and sometimes visionary ideas for making a total mess of an urban area's topography and infrastructure.

Thereministers deliver sermons by the deft waving of hands over a pulpit.

Rebutlers are servants devoted to the adroit execution of every verbal order from their masters, but never without a snide rejoinder.

Monarchaeologists excavate the graves of royalty for scientific purposes.

Kazoologists make funny noises by blowing into captive animals.

Misadventure capitalists provide start-up funds for businesses that are certain to fail catastrophically.

Gastronauts are passionate about food that is out of this world.

Vampirates are macabre nocturnal high-seas marauders who commandeer ships in order to phlebotomize innocent voyagers.

Kleptomaniactors steal scenes.

Conquistadorks invade lands but soon back out self-consciously when they realize that the people they've conquered think they're maladjusted goofs.

Janitoreadors keep bullfighting clean.

Warlocksmiths open doors and safes by casting spells.

Blandscapers are contracted to transform outdoor environments into the most innocuous and mundane settings possible.

Pornithologists use images to exploit the erotic allure of birds.

Double-crossing guards trick you into crossing the street at the most perilous moments.

Rehaberdashers purvey fine clothing for gentlemen undergoing withdrawal from addictive substances at designated facilities.

Hoboists are itinerant woodwind players whose lifestyle traditionally includes the performing of sonatas in boxcars.

Descartographers map out the mind-body dichotomy of human beings.

Global village idiots use social media to broadcast their toothless blather to the world.

Inventymologists patent new species of bugs, which seldom reach the prototype stage.

Gushers assist theatregoers to their seats in a conspicuously sycophantic manner.

Run-of-the-millwrights manufacture boring, everyday machines.

Tango-go dancers engage in melodramatic dances characterized by abrupt shifts of tempo and direction, and the gradual removal of clothes.

Sojournalists write revealing and thought-provoking articles for newspapers, blogs, and periodicals—or would, if not for being on vacation.

Repercussionists use sticks and mallets to strike drums, cymbals and other such instruments, with unfortunate musical consequences.

Blundertakers make solemn use of slapstick, miscommunication and other devices to supervise the final grim farce of a body's time on earth.

Misanthropologists are drawn to study humankind out of aversion and disgust.

Stereotypists transcribe verbal dictation while misrepresenting it in the most clichéd and simplified way possible.

Uptightrope walkers display death-defying acrobatic skills by crossing high wires in a most fretful and anxious fashion.

Obliterary agents specialize in the art of obliterature and are typically hired by authors to ensure that their works disappear without a trace and are never heard of again.

# The Tin of Fancy Excrements: A Journey of the Self

### Chapter One
### The Industrial Powder Rooms

The greyness of the city, in cold steam, draws us back to its industrial powder rooms with their blue skeletons and pneumatic tweezers, their gold-mirrored walls and coiled tubes. I thought they'd boarded up these places years ago, but we simply wandered in, unobstructed, through a doorway in the drainage tunnel behind the mall. The dust hasn't even settled onto the abattoir-like red marble countertops and Victorian dental chairs. The floors, still stained here and there with blood, are tiled in hyperrealist staircase motifs—a cruel deception for tormented souls with no path of escape. The ceilings, with their pressed-tin evil eyes, however, draw your gaze upward into a mesmeric grid of illusory surveillance.

I don't even know much about these spaces except that they were preliminary to some kind of sacrificial performance or display, and that their purpose involved cosmetic grooming. Why were so many of them required? Windowless and interconnected, these dolorous yet pristine urban catacombs serve to remind us that we know very little about even our most recent ancestors; that one generation can preserve secrets from its immediate successors; and that the value of personal hygiene and grooming—even if administered by violent strangers—is supreme in any era.

### Chapter Two
### The Burial

Striking off on my own, and changing tenses, I climbed a long narrow staircase. After exploring for some time the doorless hallway at the top, I came to a row of soft brown featureless mammals, all hanging this way and that on the grey-putty-veneered wall. Further along the purple hardwood floor, the ceiling was open to the stars, ceasing thus to be a ceiling at all.

Here I became aware of an antique odour rising, through time and space, from the tin of excrement I'd buried the week before in defiance of my beloved's wishes. I'd been outside the gates of the occult dairy. Whether I'd gone there expressly for the interment or was merely taken by the whim as I passed, I cannot recall. The tin had been in my wife's family for years. It was granted to my possession only on the condition that I return it after walking a distance sufficient to satisfy my urge. But as soon as I got the thing, I was off, like a cat with a morsel of roasted turkey dropped on the linoleum by a doddering arthritic oaf.

The burial took no more than half an hour and was watched by a lachrymose police officer whose behaviour was consistent with someone suffering from seasonal affective disorder, inoperable barometric distress syndrome, and acute male menopause. Priests from the dairy did not bother me. And suddenly the air was filled with ochre fluff. Descending and ascending, it seemed to propel me into a state of imperial contentment, as if the gods were telling me that life is pointless but I should be happy anyway and that, for what it matters, I'd done the right thing.

But how could I return home empty-handed to the tungsten and lint and cat dander of my in-laws' apartment and explain all this to the woman who'd loved me moderately for years despite my abiding desultory air and bouts of involuntary ventriloquy? She would not understand. I would simply have to flee and not look back.

That is how I came to find myself, a week later, strutting rancorously upon the recently polished floorboards of a roofless passageway leading ever on toward a mystery I didn't even care about. My aimless pilgrimage had led me, against all odds, to a place without ledges where nothing fell from the sky. I crushed a beetle in a nutcracker and wept for my sins.

### Chapter Three
### A Little Show

At 6:02 a.m. a Little Show will commence
beneath the Commodious and Redoubtable Skirts of
Larissa the Superfluous

complete with Aztec Mermaids, Hypnotized Elizabethan Emus,
Turkish Mathematicians doing Impossible Sums,
Recumbent Houseboat Contractors
and Tom the Clairvoyant Weimaraner
~ Children & Elderly welcome ~

I stared scornfully yet wistfully at the broadside and tried to scrape it off the glass of the inset fire-hose case with my fingernails, but it hung there all the more tenaciously—for whom to see? The grey putty wall had ended jaggedly just as the passageway looked like it would become too narrow to get through. I turned around to see a middle-aged man and woman, nude except for bowling shoes and vertically striped knee socks of vermillion and puce, running toward me down the hall, waving machetes. They looked possessed by ancient and malignant spirits, saliva overflowing their lower lips. It hardly seems sensible, but I waited for them to catch up with me. Their machetes carved the air ever more menacingly as they uttered quiet guttural barks. Finally, almost out of breath, they reached the spot where I stood staring in bewilderment.

My carelessness in not attempting to elude them must have spoiled their plan. They slumped, panting dreadfully, with hands on knees, the weapons still in their grip but visibly aquiver. I put a hand on the gentleman's shoulder, for he seemed to be in worse shape. Then I retracted it and wiped the sweat onto the behind of my trousers, reviled as I always am by any bodily liquids, gases, or solids issuing from another man's body. And the woman, I daren't touch, lest there appear to be prurient intent behind my action.

It was some time before they caught their breath—and I mean a very long time. My initial compassion and concern turned to boredom then consternation. Eventually they spoke, gasping and gulping as they shared the monologue:

"We may have scared you…not a little. It's…the first time we've… done it. We're…we're sweating and salivating…so much we're…getting a chill. We use Dr. Krittaways'…Spittle Pills. We're working…on a grant…from the National…Arts Foundation. We weren't intending… to actually kill…anyone. We're pleased…to meet you."

And they extended sweaty trembling hands, which I reluctantly clasped. Names were exchanged and the woman sank to her knees while the man slouched against what remained of the wall. I looked at my watch and shrugged. An announcement came over the loudspeaker system but I couldn't catch a word of it—so garbled and mean and distorted, it made my face twitch.

As they were themselves artists of some sort, I decided to share with them my visionary idea for civic improvement.

### Chapter Four
### My Idea

What I conceive of, basically, is a monument to my beloved's most ravishing blouse. To be made of burnished bronze, this extraordinary sculpture will stand approximately three storeys high in the middle of our busiest intersection. It's an idea that came to me through my higher self, guided by the ascended masters of the Far East, so please don't call it sexist. There was an exalted, numinous quality to that blouse and I'd like to see its transformative powers radiate through our fair but unenlightened city. Also, it will give me occasion to remember her form as I drive past each morning on my way to the cannery, but that's not the main reason I want it built. All that stands in the way now is the funding, and the fact that the Hopi prophecies seem to be coming true at an alarming rate. So please help us build the ravishing-blouse monument before the end of the world. We're counting on your support.

### Chapter Five
### On a Mission!

It had taken me only a few minutes to outline my proposal, yet I found upon concluding that my two new friends had fallen fast asleep, so exhausted were they by their artistic activities. At that moment, or just a moment later, my cellphone rang. It wasn't my beloved calling to say that she missed me and she didn't give a damn about the excrement, that I should just come home where I belong. No, it was someone from the Civic Iotas and Scintillas Department phoning to inform me that my lost uncle Tim-Philippe—or, as we call him, Glen—had been found and that I should go to such-and-such an address immediately.

It turns out the address was for a sluice-spigot factory a few blocks away. Upon arrival, I spoke with the foreman, a white woman, who said they'd found Glen that morning wandering through the smelting hangar with his mouth dangling open, catching sunlight. Forsaking speech, he'd attempted to communicate by dipping his fingers in a pouch of damp blue chalk and rubbing them on the skin of a tangerine. And the odd thing is, they claim to have understood him perfectly. It seems he fancies himself a highly intelligent botanical life form that just happens to resemble humans, or maybe he said it was mimicry. In any case, his expressed goal is to obtain a position as a social contractor while studying the effects of being gradually eaten alive by a vegetarian lynx he plans to keep in a closet. To this end he sought the help of those at the factory who were willing to hear of his ambition. While this was being related to me, two of the smelters wheeled him toward us on a dolly. And now, striking a fernlike pose, my uncle stood before me.

How I had the instinct to do what I did next, I've no idea. I took from my vest pocket a perforating disc, like a finely spiked pizza cutter, and ran it lightly across my uncle's left cheek. The effect was instantaneous and imperceptible. We stood almost motionless for several seconds, waiting. The drone of the machinery was beginning to loosen my muscles. At the same time, the seams of my vest and shirt were starting to rapidly unstitch, as were the seams of my trousers (I wore no boxer shorts, as they were at the dry cleaners). I slunk to the iron floor as my clothes fell from my body.

The reconnaissance mission was turning into a complete failure, but I didn't care. I felt that a freedom forbidden since early childhood, infancy perhaps, was suddenly mine again. I didn't understand a word of what was being said so far above me. An antediluvian sigh shuffled from my lips as I curled and coiled and wriggled in a foolish endocrinological pudding of objectless sensuality. Warm pee (my own, of course) flooded across my belly. All sounds were muffled as they wove together into synaesthetic orgone blankets, enveloping me in pure endorphinous comfort. Good God, was I ever relaxed! I began to laugh quietly, a whimpering blissful laugh. I knew this was the moment I'd been waiting for all my life, and it was upon me so suddenly. But then, where did it go?

The next thing I knew, I was in semi-darkness on a cold metal floor, anxious and alone. Light from a street lamp seeped in through oily yellow windowpanes, cracked by years of mediating the industrial world and nature. My ears were ringing but the vast room was silent. What remained of my clothes had been draped over me, a sweat-soaked rug barely hiding my nakedness. I shivered in a nauseous chill, teeth chattering. Tears ran from my right eye down to my left eye, then on, with the others (those originating in the left eye), to the floor. I could smell oil and rotting wood, and that was my only solace. Yet I felt strangely purified. I resolved to embrace my miserable condition and move forward into new and potentially providential states. Something marvellous was awaiting, I could feel it! Then I changed my mind and flopped back into my dreary cold malaise, confident I'd never get off the floor of the factory and never find my way out even if I did. I spent a long wretched night in foetal position, interrupted at times by spans of elegant delirium.

### Chapter Six
### A Jealous Dream

I awoke without a sound and fell over a hot cliff into a clutter of quasi-ecumenical transhuman clay, some of which was alive. Bruised, winded, scuffed, still thick with aftersleep, I watched a flock of shabby blimps trawling for skydivers and hang-gliders in a slippery turquoise sky splattered with cloudlets. There was something unswallowable about this day, something that stuck in my craw that I couldn't quite wrap my head around or put my finger on. Maybe it was the sound of those goddamned electronic church bells, wobbling toward me like a belligerent gang of flatulent basset hounds. Maybe it was the smell of cooked sewage emanating from somewhere within the gated community just beyond the claypatch. Or maybe it was just the dream I'd had. Yes—the dream. I think it was the dream...

I'd dreamt that my cherished beloved, whom I'd abandoned so impetuously, was living in a farmhouse with washed-up race-car drivers who were competing for sexual conquest of the sole female resident. This was the premise of the reality TV show being filmed by a lecherous crew of chauvinist techies bent on capturing every sanctified moment of my innocent darling's existence. Having seen part of the first episode on a high-definition widescreen television set at O'Blurmny's Pub, where I'd gone to play laser crokinole, I flew to the rescue. But upon arriving at the farm, I found myself restricted from approaching close enough to even call out to her. Physically restrained, I could do nothing but watch in jealous anguish (and of course concern for her dignity) as my precious spouse prepared to take her turn in the outdoor bathtub, beneath the pornographic gaze of dozens of macho onlookers and, ultimately, millions of television viewers.

It was at that point that I vomited myself awake and tumbled from the back of the city-bound vegetable truck onto the wet gravel of a country lane. Some stars were still visible as the morning fog drew across the sky, allowing the night to change discreetly into day.

## Chapter Seven
### Something Pleasant

By mid-afternoon—having groped my way through an increasingly familiar landscape—I reached the outskirts of the communal settlement where I'd once worked as a junior threat detector and eco-semiologist. I knew I could get some clothes there and a bite to eat, and it would be an ideal place for yet another change of tense.

I'm soon greeted by the paramilitary neo-hippie security squad, who welcome me with open arms of both types (fortunately they miss with both). After leading me into camp, they give me a perfectly ripe avocado and a pair of standard-issue violet-and-taupe overalls. I check into one of the canvas enclosures that serve as living quarters for guests.

It's implausibly dark in my tent, even with the curtains torn off and worn as kilts by the marauding mandrills, their garishly sexy bottoms—what was God thinking!—covered at last. The dimness makes it easier to nap, so I do, but not for long because I want to be on my way again before nightfall.

Leaving the tent, I stroll toward the hillside stairway I used to climb now and again during my sojourn at the camp, when I was off-duty. I happen to be joined by a charming young woman I've never met—likely one of the new breed of geo-linguists who travel from settlement to settlement. Clouds break and the afternoon gloominess gives way to sudden brilliance.

As we ascend the hillside stair of old tongues, pelts and feathers, I say, "I always like going up here, because there's always something pleasant on the other side."

She smiles wanly, then, when she thinks I'm not looking, curls her upper lip and rolls her eyes in a kind of okay-mister-if-you-say-so expression—no doubt recalling the corporeal atrocities she's seen just over the hill on other excursions.

*Right,* I remember. *It's never pleasant at all!* I was suddenly aware that my mind had created false memories to mask the grisly impressions scarred into my brain on previous ascents.

We rise a few steps more.

"You know," I say. "I just remembered there's a baby meadow vole that needs to be bottle-fed back at the encampment. Maybe I should…"

She nods and smiles, like a mother who's just caught her youngest tax consultant's pet owl in a leg trap.

Back down in the valley, I see a shimmering geodesic dome that wasn't there when I left for the stairs. Its gossamer skin ripples in the breeze. As I near, I see that this covering appears to have been made by spiders—large, fast spiders. The web is so intricate and light as to dazzle all retinal and rational expectations. I get too close and breathe a hole in it, then the damn thing collapses, quilliferous lattice and all.

I'm not having much luck today. Maybe I should head into town.

### Chapter Eight
### In a Strange Town

After a quick smoked-pickerel sandwich (which happens to be outstanding), I leave the settlement on foot and amble down into a meandering ravine that leads, in my memory, to a monorail station at the perimeter of the city. But the deeper I wander into this lush slash across the landscape, the more religiously, existentially and (worst of all) physically lost I become. A butterfly lands on my forearm and bites me fiercely until I bleed. I'm too squeamish about guts to squash it, but I certainly didn't expect the brutish laceration it inflicts. Nor did I expect the sight that lies beyond the next curve of the ravine—though I could swear I saw it once in a dream.

Spread out before me is a town of modest size sitting in a valley scooped out at the terminus of the ravine. It seems typical of many other villages I've seen that date from the late 1800s or so, except for one thing—or rather many things, all of which are water towers. Why would one small town need so many elevated water-storage structures? The question hardly crosses my mind, for I am swept away by their benign and lofty majesty as they loom imperiously over the churches and factories, the houses, schools, and shops of the town. It is as if all the water towers of the world have been assembled to astound me. I descend the verdant slope of mown grass to walk among this forest of architectural marvels, each tower distinct: here a futuristic ovoid steel column; there a modernist brick obelisk; in the distance a classical concrete pillar. A brooding gothic megalith might neighbour a sleek minimalist spindle; an imposing archaeo-industrial needle might stand aflank a neo-romantic ivory tower.

There are people in this town, but always in the distance. No one is ever close enough for me to ask the name of the place, and any sign I see—though they all appear to be in English—is curiously incomprehensible, as though a sort of letterform virus or sensorial glitch has rendered the whole of its typography illegible.

So I wander in this strange town, alone in my serene astonishment, down empty streets of eroding asphalt painted with the shadows of monolithic wonders.

In a cul-de-sac at the end of a placid residential street, as eerily deserted as the others, stands an elegant cylinder of pre-stressed concrete that fans outward toward its top, twenty or so metres in the air. There are vertically elongated windows of lapis blue glass high up on its shaft. On either side of it extends a tall hedge obscuring the view beyond.

A small dog—a dwarf Appalachian terrier, I think—dashes onto the road and rolls onto its back at my feet, wanting to be petted.

I scruffle it behind the ears and tickle its tummy before resuming my approach to the tower. The pup seems satisfied and does not follow.

At the cream-coloured tower's base is an archway the size of a door. The salty smell of the sea greets me as I enter the tunnel. In the short time it takes me to reach the far opening, twilight has fallen. The clouds, in striated mounds, are purple and orange above the sea.

With the mysterious town at my back, I walk across the sand until, about a half-kilometre along its granular expanse, I arrive at a vacant beach gazebo with the number 3 painted in violet pink on its roof. This day, like all others, has been long. It's time for another of my naps. And where better to nap than in the cozy seaside confines of Gazebo No. 3?

## Chapter Nine
## The Night Picnic

It is nighttime and there is a sickening volley of *glorps* emanating from the soggy sands beside the pier, where wet delinquents pirouette into the frothy drink. There must be something horrid over there on the drenched beach—something the fuzzy glow of flying saucers has failed to illuminate. The sound is, perhaps, that of some invisible nastiness, such as a sasquatchean ghost plucking giant crabs from their saturated embedments. I can think of nothing else that could make such a harrowing nocturnal concerto.

Let us turn our thoughts away from this unsolvable mystery that so perturbs me, if it's all the same to you, and cast our perceptual net across the other length of the strand, where fiercely cheerful picnics have broken out at the foot of grand mammarian dunes lit by the arabesque flight paths of fireflies drunk with summer lust. There, beneath torches shaded in gloxinia blue and canopies striped in persimmon and aubergine, our revellers dine on fresh-caught shellfish barbecued over hallucinogenic embers. It seems that nothing could disturb the easy humour of these rakishly hairy men and brashly sensuous women, celebrating life together beneath the approving constellations that glitter to match each twinkle in their jovial Atlantean eyes. What a welcome sight this is to you who have just begun your travels on this night and I who have been wandering for days.

As this scene grows closer with each footfall, our hearts soar to match the good spirits of our neighbours, into whose company we will soon be welcomed as fellow lovers of life.

But wait! They've spotted us and are charging this way with their shucking blades and fish-gutting knives! Quick—onto that abandoned speedboat! Oh, damn, the motor won't start! Dear God, there must be something to throw, or something to— There! The gasoline! Grab that can of... Huh? They're laughing at us? They've stopped just short of massacring us and are having a damn good laugh at our expense. Very funny. Ha-ha-ha. That's it—wipe the tears away and go back to your bloody picnic, you twisted bastards. Yeah, that's it—moon us, you creepy broads. God, you'd think I would have learned by now. I guess I was bound to fall for it sooner or later. Do I ever need a tranquilizer. Well, enough of this. No more roaming among the psychos for me. I'm going home.

## Chapter Ten
### Back Home at Last, I Await the New Age

Leeches on damp trees, spongiferous clouds clotting the horizon, a tube of eyeshadow dropped from the purse of a hang-gliding Corporate Expungements Officer, a spider's web shimmering between a nude woman's sleeping corgis: these are the things of which the dawn is made (along with bashed letters, a gilded furnace pipe, and three milking dollies lying aslant in the tousled ditches alongside Highway 402 about three kilometres west of the turnoff to Watford).

All this splendour—a veritable pornutopia of overlooked objects ready to be found and labelled by some fresh goal-oriented mind—and I can't seem to find my way out of bed. A compass and an ice pick would be useful, I'm sure, as would 130 milligrams of pure caffeine in the form of boiled potable water poured over a tablespoon of ground and filtered pre-roasted coffee beans—now, why is that illegal!—but all I have is this pen and paper, and, as every schoolchild who read *A Colloquy of Grievances* knows, I couldn't write myself out of a wet paper bag let alone a bed of this strength and vastness. There must be a way to bring the world to me—some kind of inner net that could be projected outward to encircle the globe, capturing even the least predictable objects: flashing horse brassieres, cellphone toupées, electric face slappers and more—much, much more. Voracious engines could search for whatever I desire, load it onto the net and send it hurtling toward me at furious speed, only for it to stop an instant before impact, right at my fingertips. Such technology may still be several months away, but I'm willing to wait. I will be in this bed, according to my latest calculations, until the Thirteenth Baktun dwindles away and the shadow of the plumed serpent descends the stone steps of Chichen Itza. I will be here until the local garbage bylaws change and free men and women are allowed to throw out whatever they want whenever they want. Prone, I will lie, with my blindfold and comforter and foam-rubber pillow, until the bargains become unbeatable and a new age dawns.

## Beautiful Thoughts

Clear
your mind

of all thoughts

except
the ones

you are currently

thinking

•

There is
nothing

you can't
become

so don't even bother

not becoming

everything

•

Always be kind
to strangers:

you never know
when you might meet
the Buddha
in disguise

or some
asshole
who's going
to report
you

•

It comes
screaming down
the centuries
to greet us

and we're never
home

when
it arrives

•

There is
a universe

in which
I iron

the same
pair of pants

over and over again

forever

•

We've got
enough bombs
to blow up
the world
a hundred times

and yet

we don't
have the guts
to do it

•

One word
is not enough

to say that

one word
is enough

•

She refused
to buy

baby oil

because
she thought
it was

inhumane

•

He chose to live
in the nineteenth century

and they could find
no law
against it

•

Most things

don't happen

•

*Mommy*

said the enraptured
little girl

*I want to climb up
every drainpipe
in the world!*

•

It has now
been

over seven hours

since I began

writing this
sentence

•

One needs one's
higher faculties

to determine

whatever it is
one is doing

down there

on the floor

•

If you can
hear these words

outside of
your head

call the number

on the back
of your radio

•

The
brain
is a
chrysalis

•

The sky

isn't what you
think it is

.

He took
his time-lapse capsules
and watched

the boat race

from an unfinished
bridge

.

Her new hairdo

is as dainty

as an amoeba's
orgasm

.

We washed
all their movies
down the
train

.

The overindulgent
pop star

died

in a pool
of his own

design

.

This story
has seventy-six
characters—

the type
you wouldn't

want to read

in a dark
alley

.

It turned out
she was just a
product

of her own

imagination

.

A heavy smoker
he one day
just collapsed
at free fall
into his own
footprint

•

Nature
has gone
wild

we're going
to have to
teach it

a lesson

•

*Wholesome Goodness*™

from the people

who'd rather
see you

dead

•

O ye
of little
evidence!

•

I'm sorry—
there's been
a mistake:

those weren't
the days

after all

•

After his
meteoric rise to
obscurity

he went down
in mystery

•

Tonight
she is
sad

she is

all over

the world

•

Build an engine
with words

let it make you
speak

# David McFadden Trip
## (A Reminiscence on the Occasion of the Seventieth Birthday of the Author of *A Trip Around Lake Ontario* and Many Other Marvellous Travelogues, Memoirs, and Collections of Poetry)

I'd always wanted to join David McFadden on one of his trips, so when I happened to mention a place I'd been reading about that sounded quite interesting and he suggested we go, I was delighted.

"By the way," he asked, "is it far?"

"Unfathomably," I replied, "according to the guidebooks."

"So how long do you think it will take to get there?"

"Well, about twelve to fifteen seconds, depending on traffic."

"And how long will we stay?"

"Dave," I said, "we're not applying for a travel grant, let's just keep it open. But at the most, say, six or seven minutes. It's an amazing place, apparently, lots to see—but most people say a relatively short visit is all you need. Or can handle," I added, hoping to further intrigue his adventurous spirit. It worked.

"Sounds great," he said. "Let's go!"

It was a Thanksgiving evening, toward the end of the second millennium. The restaurant owed me some time off so I'd managed to clear my schedule all the way until the following morning.

As I awaited Dave's arrival, I reflected on another Thanksgiving a couple years earlier, or perhaps later. On that occasion, Dave was to join my family for turkey dinner at our apartment. Never having been there, he got lost en route and was considerably delayed. To be fair, the apartment was underground, and its address *was* displayed in roman numerals, and I *may* have inadvertently used Cockney rhyming slang when I told him the name of the street, but surely his Taoist instincts could have led him to our door before the gravy got cold. If I were to fictionalize the event, I would have my wife say something like "He can find his way around the Great Lakes, no problem, but finding his way across town to our apartment seems quite beyond him." The truth is, I don't remember what she did say, or even, with any certainty, what she didn't. For that matter, I don't recall how Dave finally ended up at our place—this was prior, obviously, to mandatory GPS implants—but I do recall that he was splendid company. Dinner conversation revolved around gerunds, and at the end of the evening we all felt charmed and illuminated by his presence.

But that was well before, or after, the evening that concerns us: October 11, 1993, to be precise. Or perhaps 1994.

Dave arrived around 8:12, right on time and ready for our trip. My friends from B.C. had loaned me a vehicle especially for the excursion—an odd two-seater they'd nicknamed the "Dymaxion Model T." We carefully packed it for the journey, making sure we'd remembered not to bring anything, and were soon sitting side by side with a shared sense of wonder and trepidation.

"Shall we take turns driving?" asked Dave.

"Splendid idea."

With a "here goes" sort of glance to my travel companion, I cranked the ignition, closed my eyes, and in no time at all we were off in a cloud of smoke.

"That's a good book," observed the sagely stranger as he drifted past me on the otherwise empty subway platform. "I've been there."

I was absorbed in an obscure tome about the ancient Arthurian mysteries of Glastonbury Tor and environs—which I hoped to explore during an upcoming trip to England—when suddenly this Merlinesque being materialized out of nowhere to affirm my spiritual quest. That he may have simply transferred from the Bloor line made his presence no less remarkable. Magician or apparition, I determined not to let him slip away before I could at least ask a question or two. Who knew, perhaps this was my guru, offering one chance to recognize him and further my path toward revelation. But after catching him up and chatting for a moment or two I realized that, no—despite his obvious wisdom and benign nature—maybe he was, after all, just some guy on the subway. And yet there was something uncannily familiar about this individual who was so comfortably uncommon in his bearing. Not to say there was anything the least bit outlandish in his appearance: that he gave the impression of wearing a cape without actually wearing one seemed to be part of his nature. Clearly I was in the presence of a rare intellect, one so accustomed to generating synchronicities of this nature that he could abide them with nonchalance—quite happy to discuss the latest speculations on the geomantic zodiac of the Somerset landscape with me but somehow imparting the sense that his day had already been quite rich enough with young men interrogating him on the subject. It so happened that we both disembarked at Dupont Station, just down the street and across town from where we would set off on a journey together one Thanksgiving evening four or five years hence—for this curious outsider, it finally dawned on me after we'd shaken hands and parted, was none other than David McFadden.

I'd known of McFadden since I was a teenager, scanning the local library shelves for the most unusual Canadian poetry I could find. Later, after crossing the plains of Southwestern Ontario to settle in Toronto at age twenty, I got to experience his work first-hand. There were many fine readings to attend that summer of 1982, and the best ones tended to feature the author of *The Ova Yogas* and *My Body Was Eaten by Dogs* reading poems such as "Thirty-Four Lines About Horses" to an eager audience that hung on his every—how shall I put it?—word. Thanks to a bit of luck, I even got a chance to read on the same bill as McFadden, way before I ever knew how to pronounce *mollusk* let alone write a decent poem. But that bearded short-haired McFadden was different from the clean-shaven long-haired bespectacled McFadden I'd encountered in the underground. Here was a hero with, if not a thousand, at least a couple faces.

This is not the place to recount how I eventually became permanently acquainted with David W. McFadden. That story, I'm sure, will form a captivating chapter in the biography he's writing about me. Or was that a dream? How embarrassing—that was just a dream. In any case, I really should get back to that night when we returned home from our trip in the Dymaxion Model T.

It was still light out when we got back to my apartment, which is odd because the sun had set around two hours earlier. I paced excitedly across the living-room carpet, but Dave was content to recline on the floor with his back against the sofa. He had a beguiled look on his face, like a mathematician who'd just been told a new species of horse had been named after him. As for myself, I was in a state of astonishment bordering on what Jules Verne's translator might call "stupefaction."

"My God! I knew from the brochures that it was a unique spot, but...who could have imagined! Why isn't this place on the news every day? Maybe it's just so astounding people can't believe it actually exists, even after they've been there. Or maybe its attractions are too terrific, in every sense, for the average tourist to withstand. Do you suppose that's why it's not an approved destination—that the government is protecting us from exposure to the marvellous? Or is it just that it's so extraordinary, so full of secrets, that they don't want us to even talk about it? I mean, did you see that...that...?"

"I saw it, all right," said Dave. "I saw it all. I'm just not sure what any of it was."

"So you're not going to write about it?" I asked, secretly fancying myself a character in one of his literary adventures.

He seemed, for a moment, to ponder how he might go about writing a travel narrative about our strange little vacation. His steady gaze focused on something only he could see, and as he turned toward me I noticed a slight but dramatic billowing of his invisible cloak.

"Sometimes," came the answer of my guru, my friend, "it's good to be just a tourist."

# Plight of the Urban Sasquatch and Other Limericks

There is no easy way for a sasquatch to mate
His fondest of hopes is a very blind date
But the moment she smells him
The gal always tells him
*Pardon me, sir, I must absquatulate*

•

There once was a man from Southampton
Who couldn't care less what he camped on
So he set up his tent
On a strip of cement
And when rush hour came he got stamped on

•

The cat is a creature of habit
If a mouse draws in sight it will grab it
With eyes sharp as lasers
And claws sharp as razors
It will fix on its prey and then jab it

•

Now the snow is falling nice and soft
I watch it from the window of my loft
Some folks would call it a garret
But I couldn't give a shit where it
Is from whence I watch the snowflakes waft

•

There once was a drug called caffeine
Prized for turning moods pleasant from mean
And any old dolt
Who experienced its jolt
Could suddenly think like Einstein

•

If it falls from the sky with a clunk
And it doesn't melt, flutter, or plunk
What you've got on your hands
Or wherever it lands
Is more likely than not…space junk

•

The lord is my shepherd, I've got all I want:
A cut by Sassoon and a dress by Ms. Quant!
Now, I don't mean to boast
But I must make a toast:
To that saviour who made me a true bon vivant!

•

There once was a dog with three eyes
Who took great delight catching flies
Whene'er one alighted
This dog triply sighted
Emitted a flurry of sighs

•

Two birds with one stone I can easily see
But three stones with two birds seems a mystery
So when it comes to ballistics
Please explain the logistics
When planes there were two but towers three

94

·

The words are helpless to resist
The hand that shapes them from the mist
Of mental vales
Where nightingales
Serenade the...well, you get the gist

·


The writers of these are oft thought to be sick
Or at best sad specimens of word lunatic
Whose affliction or virus
Will always require us
To suffer the recital of their latest five-line rhyming poem

# Beyond Me

They can put a man on the moon, and yet they can't seem to keep dogs from crapping on sidewalks.

They can paint a picture of a Campbell's soup can and call it art, and yet they can't seem to solve the problems in the Middle East.

They can tell the day you were born by looking at a piece of paper, and yet they can't seem to find the Loch Ness monster.

They can make a hole in the ozone, and yet nine times out of ten they can't seem to poach an egg the way you want it.

They can sell magazines with bare-breasted women on the cover, and yet they can't seem to provide enough shelter for the homeless.

They can make a pill that keeps you awake all night, and yet they can't seem to prevent drought in poor countries.

They can fill an entire football stadium with people, and yet they can't seem to design an umbrella that doesn't end up getting lost sooner or later.

They can run around the world killing princesses and blowing up towers, and yet they can't seem to keep people from sticking chewing gum under restaurant tables.

They can design a car that runs on gasoline, and yet they can't seem to halt the merciless sorcery of time, which transforms, with excruciating slowness, babies into grizzled geriatrics so far removed from their original state they can barely recognize themselves.

They can split the atom, and yet they can't seem to make a decent film adaptation of a Jules Verne novel.

They can medicate a man in such a way that the erectile tissue of his genital shaft becomes engorged and stiffens to facilitate participation in sexual pastimes or even copulation with the aim of inseminating his wife, and yet they can't seem to keep the streets free of litter.

They can bring your ancestors back from the dead, and yet they can't seem to make a toaster that's easy to clean.

They can build a giant machine to control the weather and set off earthquakes, and yet they can't seem to get the stains off the Shroud of Turin.

They can find a bunch of bones in the earth and put them together in the shape of a dinosaur, and yet they can't seem to find a way to end fighting in hockey.

# Incidents of Exposure: Preliminary Annual Report

A man exposed himself on a roof in Lansing, Michigan, after chasing a squirrel with a broken broom.

Three perfumists exposed themselves, somewhere in Rhode Island, while walking one another's dogs.

Two maintenance workers at the Edmonton Valley Zoo, in their off-hours, exposed themselves for charity during a visit by one of the lesser British royals.

Anita Carsten, a white stenographer from North America, exposed herself. She was thirty-four.

Seven paramedics in training exposed themselves sequentially while performing a reverse-psychology exercise relating to false seizures (San Francisco, U.S.A.).

An astronaut on the old space station claimed to have exposed himself but in fact had not.

Four individuals of various sexes exposed themselves inadvertently while chatting in the window of a Rochester, New York, coffee shop (topics were vitamins and baboons). Incident was witnessed, though not reported, by an unemployed snowplow operator who'd just left a nearby bar upon finding out he wasn't welcome.

Eighteen parachuting hedonists (the name of their club and whereabouts has been accidentally erased) exposed themselves twice under group hypnosis.

Four male shepherds, from various places in the U.K., exposed themselves on webcam in a futile effort to deflect attention from their hunger strike.

A streetwalker in Gdansk, Poland, exposed herself due to relatively high winds and an apparent wardrobe malfunction.

A Peruvian air-traffic controller and her trainee exposed themselves when they were unable to take lunch because of the high volume of flights in Lima on that particular day (the reasons for which were perfectly clear at the time, but have since been forgotten).

A member of the Huli tribe of Papua New Guinea exposed himself one Thursday afternoon.

Five house painters, on two separate jobs in an unknown Bulgarian town, exposed themselves simultaneously and without prior communication.

A bacteriologist is rumoured to have exposed himself (no details available).

Two political canvassers in Brampton, Ontario—one an Anglo-Saxon male, the other a veterinary student—exposed themselves in the doorway of a private residence that happened to belong to a radio show host who'd just done a program on the aftermath of the 2010 exposures in neighbouring Caledon (which turned out to be a combination of hoax and mass hysteria).

A wading-pool attendant in Vincennes, Indiana, exposed herself nine times during a fourteen-day span, setting a new world record and leading to her appointment as campaign manager of a local candidate's ultimately unsuccessful bid for the mayoralty.

## Some Common and Not-So-Common Similarities

Weasels are like husbands: they wear tweed coats and pop out of nowhere in the night.

Zeitgeists are like pomegranates: no one knows where they come from, and it's not always worth the effort to dissect them.

Houndstooth patterns are like abandoned symphonies: in most cases we're better off without them.

Persimmons are like the Canary Islands: I always forget what they are.

Sex between, or among, consenting adults is like candy floss: a little bit will make you sick, but after a certain amount you hardly notice it and wonder why you didn't try it sooner.

Sports scores are like afternoon seances: the level of abstraction is breathtaking.

A quiet drive in the country is like a shoehorn: if all goes right, you'll be up and about again before you know it.

Studio musicians—even mediocre ones—are like eavestroughs: you spend all your time staring at them when you could be doing other things.

Reclining chairs are like skyscrapers: once they're up, you might as well leave them like that.

Collecting Iron Age statuary is like keeping a Vietnamese pot-bellied pig as a pet: it's great at first but then…time to move on!

The sands of the hourglass are like the dials on a computer: you know they're there for a reason, you just can't imagine what it might be.

Strangers encountered by chance are like the calm before the storm: no definition until after the fact.

Predilections for avocados are like two-faced liars: if you humour them but keep them under control, no one needs to know a thing.

Conventions for catapult enthusiasts are like dachshunds: if you haven't read the manual, you might as well forget it.

The White Cliffs of Dover are like honey: best when hard!

Binoculars are like sheep: turn them the wrong way and you'll get a surprise.

The lives of others are like dowsing rods: try getting by without either one, and you'll see what I mean.

Syntax is like the memory of a terrible nightmare brought on by stress about the state of the world: you can think about it for as long as you want, but nothing will change until you look in the mirror and ask yourself, *Why does it have to be this way?*

Searching for answers is like a motor with no moving parts: it won't put bread on the table, but what's the harm?

Desire is like water: you can put it in a bottle and fly it around the world, but it still drives you up the wall.

Interplanetary travel is like finding something you didn't pay for at the bottom of your grocery bag: just enjoy it for what it is and let others worry about the ramifications.

Maintaining consciousness is like a red wheelbarrow: if you ask the experts, everything depends on it.

Skydiving on an empty stomach is like amnesia: the moment you open your mouth, it's already too late.

Toxic flowers are like good friends: if you bite them, no one will think twice about it.

Libraries are like melancholy children: they're fine for what they are, but nothing will ever replace a good bowel movement.

Vanity is like a replica tortoise made out of porcelain: the one time you want to show somebody, it's nowhere to be found.

Doppelgängers are like broken Jacuzzis: both have been the subject of novellas, and neither one reacts to thunderclaps.

A piece of cake is like a walk in the park: play your cards right and it won't be your last.

Clean, wet Formica® is like a house on stilts: besides the obvious, it's almost certain that both have been admired at some point or another by dragonflies.

A lunar eclipse is like the first time you see a dog drink from a toilet bowl: it's kind of freaky, but everything returns to normal afterwards.

Butterflies are like enemas: if you make enough money, you can have all you want.

# Other News

In other news, President Kennedy was shot dead today while on his way to a business luncheon in Dallas, Texas.

And now here's Andrew with sports.

In other news, humans landed on the moon for the first time in history earlier today. The spectacle was marred when American astronaut Neil Armstrong flubbed his lines in front of 125 million television viewers. As he stepped tentatively onto the lunar soil, the distracted NASA employee said it was "One small step for Man" rather than "One small step for *a* man," as intended. Befuddled viewers must have wondered at the paradox when Armstrong, in the same breath, referred to the occasion as "One giant leap for Mankind." Better dust off that résumé when you get back to Earth, Neil!

And now here's Darya with this evening's lottery numbers.

In other news, a forty-seven-storey steel office tower in New York collapsed at free fall into its own footprint late this afternoon, baffling architects and structural engineers worldwide. Office fires were said to be the cause of the collapse, making it the first such occurrence in history. There were no injuries as the building had already been evacuated. Earlier in the day, two other skyscrapers collapsed after being struck by planes. Several thousand people are believed to have perished in that horrific double tragedy.

And now over to Ken for a special report on securing your tulip bulbs against pesky squirrels this autumn. Ken?

In other news, the wreckage of a flying saucer has been found near Roswell, New Mexico, along with the bodies of several extraterrestrial crew members. One of the diminutive visitors is said to be alive but rather shaken up by the incident. I think I might be a bit shaken up too if I found myself stranded in rural New Mexico with no means of— Wait a moment, I'm getting an update. According to U.S. Air Force officials, it was just a weather balloon. Well, isn't that a humorous twist. Any witnesses who might claim they saw something other than a weather balloon are being advised to kindly keep quiet or risk death to themselves and their families.

And speaking of weather, here's Cathy with the facts on what *we* can expect to see falling from the sky. Take it away, Cathy.

In other news, to the delight of His followers, Jesus Christ returned to Earth today in a blaze of glory. When pressed for a comment, the beloved prophet of the Christian faith said He was glad to be back but had a lot of work ahead of Him. Those who doubted the saviour's "second coming" will be hearing a lot of *I told you so*'s for the next week or two!

And now here's Safira with the latest on traffic.

In other news, the Toronto Maple Leafs won their fourteenth Stanley Cup this evening after a drought of nearly two centuries when they defeated the San Juan Chupacabras 4-3 in overtime at the Walmart Penitentiary Arena. Sadly for diehard fans, their celebration will be short-lived, as an asteroid struck the earth just moments later—an event expected to terminate most forms of life on the planet by next Tuesday (Friday at the latest).

And now here's Zorguloxina-32 with the scoop on this virtual summer's fashion trends.

# Reflection of a Hole

I once saw the reflection[1]
of a hole.
So young was I then,
so resolute in my
doleful glimmering.

The grace of this lifetime
is that I have grown more
frivolous with age, have
seen all my closets repainted
a dozen times or more
by elderly boys and girls
who come unbidden
at any hour of the day,
singly or in pairs (at least once
as a trio), without my consent,
in colours I neither chose
nor knew existed.

I once saw
the reflection of a hole—
though it may have been
the shadow of a coffee spoon,
teased to breaking by
a prankster kettle
whose mirrorous convexity
caught my child-gaze
and met it unfazed,
stretching a world I
barely knew all out
of shape—like a
magician whose only
so-called trick is to
punch you in the stomach.

And yet, I'm pretty sure
that somewhere
there was a hole.

---

1. A poem that requires a footnote in the first line is often doomed from
the outset.

# Distended Aphorisms

There's a time and a place for everything, but it's not now and it's certainly not here.

Everybody has to pay the piper, but you might not have to pay him much if he happens to be non-union.

Tomorrow is a new day, but the day after that has been made up of recycled moments you were too busy and depressed to notice.

Intelligence is the ultimate aphrodisiac, but a dab of extract from a civet's anal gland and a nice pair of shoes will usually work just as well.

What goes around comes around, but don't expect to get any of it unless you've already got too much.

Where there's a will there's a way, but where there's no will there's no way you're going to get anything more than a set of commemorative plates and a busted footstool.

Rome wasn't built in a day, but that was before they invented drywall.

The Lord works in strange and mysterious ways, but then so do serial killers and plumbers.

Laughter is the best medicine, but I'll still take the intravenous Demerol if it's all the same to you.

Some people try to be tall by cutting off the heads of others, but they're usually apprehended within a few hours.

The road to Hell is paved with good intentions, but I never believe those travel brochures.

Poetry is compensation for the miseries we endure, but that doesn't mean I'm going to drop the lawsuit.

To the pessimist the glass is half empty and to the optimist it's half full, but to the paying customer it's a rip-off no matter how you look at it.

A woman's work is never done, but if you do happen to take a break, do you think you could grab me a beer?

When the Lord closes a door He opens a window and when He closes a window He opens a door, but if He keeps that up all night I'll have Him evicted.

Time heals all wounds, but if I were you I'd see a doctor just the same.

You have to break a few eggs to make an omelette, but you only have to break one to make a baby.

Life is a tale told by an idiot, full of sound and fury, but death is a short certificate written by a sensible fellow with a degree in forensic pathology.

Pissing in one's shoes will not keep one's feet warm for long, but it's a surefire way to get out of a bad date.

There is no excellent beauty that hath not some strangeness in the proportion, but I'm just saying that to make you feel good.

## Manta Ray Jack and the Crew of the *Spooner*
### *An Undignified Sea Tour*

Upon climbing the steps of the lighthouse, Shauna—unaccustomed to such horrid flights and florid heights—quavered wheezily and wavered queasily atop the last gleaming stair. Beside her, in the steaming glare, loomed the sentry—a veering sniper with the look of a sneering viper. From above their heads, the focused light in the idle tower shone with the intensity of a locust fight in the tidal hour.

Far below, where sea grazed coast, the creeping beam wandered like a crazed ghost, lighting in the livid purview of its vivid purlieu a series of seaside scenes, to wit: a mock duck and a dairy fox covered in dock muck on the ferry docks; a brash hick hawking his wares (a hash brick) while walking his hares; a fawn buyer and a lane mobster at a bonfire eating Maine Lobster™ (*"hand-caught and canned hot!"*); a cab driver and a crab diver discussing the tipping of rides and the ripping of tides; a skinny troll with a musty funk stealing a tinny scroll from a fusty monk; two glamorous imps exchanging an amorous glimpse after pining in the dark while dining in the park; and a pretty girl

---

## Manta Ray Jack and the Crew of the *Spooner*
### *An Unsignified Detour*

Upon climbing the steps of the lighthouse, Shauna—unaccustomed to such terribly long stairways and extravagant elevations—experienced a trembling asthmatic shortness of breath and an oscillating nausea as she stood atop the final sparkling step. Beside her, in the hazy aureola of the edifice's incandescent pinnacle, loomed the sentry—an unsteady sharpshooter with the look of a poisonous snake whose features have been constricted into a contemptible grin. From above their heads, the source of radiance within the still, columnar structure cast its sharply defined beam with all the force of a battle among large swarming grasshoppers at a point in the day when the sea rises or falls due to the gravitational influence of the moon and sun, or perhaps at some cataclysmic juncture in a history not yet known to man or so long past as to be lost from collective awareness.

Far below, where ocean met shore, the sweeping luminosity meandered like an insane spectre, lighting on its way the following seaside scenes: a mallard decoy and a lactophilic canid enslimed on a pier from which a small carrier boat makes its regular voyage to a nearby island and back; a bold rustic lad selling a resinous psychoactive block while exercising his bunnies; a purchaser of young female deer and an alley gangster at a controlled outdoor blaze eating delectable

with a Yorkie puppy admiring a gritty pearl with a porky yuppie. Also visible in the roving light was a sprawl of schoonerists whose ship, now docked, was covered in the scrawl of spoonerists.

Spotting something extraordinary in the curling waves, Shauna (still a dusty wreck from her recent travels through whirling caves), clutched the rusty deck's white rail and exclaimed, "A right whale!"

"That's no whale," replied the sentry, "just a thievious dunderhead with a spine fin."

A devious thunderhead with a fine spin clouded the starry sky while, beneath its swervish dimming, an odd fellow in a dolphin costume splashed about like a dervish swimming.

"I'd know that vapid Raleigh anywhere, even with the fishy disguise," continued the sentry. "He once stole my parking space."

As lightning began to flash at a sparking pace, he aimed his trusty rifle—a deadly if rusty trifle—and fired a rapid volley at the descendant of Sir Wally (an English adventurer who once lost his head in a royal folly: the only sure way, it seemed, to foil Raleigh).

Shauna, prone to nausea, hobbled then whirled as her guts wobbled then hurled. Having recently lost her dear father Fred and

---

canned crustacean meat from the east coast of the USA; a taxi operator and an underwater hunter of certain other tasty carapacious life forms gabbing to each other about gratuity protocol and hazardous currents; a slender and dankly odorous cave-dwelling gnome absconding with a metallic roll of parchment belonging to a stuffy, old-fashioned member of an insular male spiritual commune; a couple of alluringly chic mischievous sprites expressing libidinal inclinations, each toward the other, at the conclusion of a repast within the perimeter of a public green space; and an attractive young woman holding a baby Yorkshire terrier while observing, in the company of a chubby urban professional, the beauty of a sandy but lustrous accretion manufactured by an otherwise unindustrious aquatic bivalve. Another thing revealed by the traversing beam was the haphazardly dispersed crew of a schooner at anchor, which appeared to be decorated in the graffiti of dyslexics.

A little grimy and worse for wear after her recent journey, the itinerary of which involved egress into a series of somehow twirling underground chambers, Shauna sighted something unusual at a distance and became excited. Clasping the protective barrier around the lookout platform—far less pristine than its adjoining staircase—she turned to the sentry and breathlessly shared the discovery of what she thought to be a species of cetacean once almost hunted to extinction. As a mischievous storm cloud exhibiting fledgling cyclonic proclivities obscured the

mother Alison-Beth in ghastly ways—her father had been gored to death by a bull and her mother bored to death by a gull—she had hoped her vacation would be relatively free of fear, bother, dread, and other malice and death.

"Anyway," opined the sheepish potshot crack-head killer like a creepish crackpot hothead shiller, "he made a piss-poor porpoise, if you ask me."

Then, with rather less justification, he shot the gormless fool who'd rushed to the water's edge like a formless ghoul to wave the sail that read *SAVE THE WHALE!*

Taking a restorative breath of the night's charmed air, Shauna withdrew into the lighthouse and sank into a comfortably armed chair.

Moments later, the skipper of the schooner ascended and made his entrance, setting on the coffee table the gift of a crude shrew kept for just such an occasion by his shrewd crew. Curiously enough there was a tame sable on the same table.

"We couldn't help but notice that your light was on," announced the captain, "so we thought we'd nop in for a dribble." He went on to

---

constellated heavens, the sentry (who could, by the way, be classified as a hangdog murderer fond of taking random shots at unprotected targets while subject to the effects of a cheap but highly addictive stimulant derived from coca leaves and smoked in a glass pipe) explained that what Shauna had spotted was actually just a stupid swindler wearing a dorsal flipper as part of a disguise. The sentry further identified him by the name of Raleigh, thus genealogically linking this man floundering toward shore in a dolphin costume with one Sir Walter, a venturesome Elizabethan courtier celebrated for sticking his neck out for his country in diverse and exceptional ways.

Stroboscopic electrical discharges from the cumulonimbus formation foreshadowed, or were at least a precursor of, the quick succession of bullets fired from the sentry's long-barrelled assault gun at the hapless figure below.

This vicious display of unwarranted brutality was enough to make poor Shauna—who, orphaned under unpleasant and unusual circumstances, had been hoping for a vacation void of gruesome slaying—lose whatever equilibrium she'd gained and vomit over the ivory guardrail of the observation deck.

The sentry's only comment on his horrendous act was that, in his opinion, the victim—whose sole crime against him was once having beaten him to a parking space—hadn't made a very convincing marine mammal.

Then—merely because he thought him dimwitted, it seems—he also shot

explain that he and his sailors, who'd risen in his wake and now stood listening intently like a gaggle of capped runts, had been voyaging to Malaysia to enjoy some teriyaki bluefin halibut in a very tacky flu-bin Bali hut notorious for its mystic fillets and fistic melees.

"The perfect place," he noted, "for both a whitefish and a fight wish! But," continued the seadog as he began to de-sog from the tiny shower that had befallen his ship as it neared the shiny tower, "on our way to get a Bali tan we were ji-hacked by the Taliban. There we were, you see, minding our biz and binding our mizz—our mizzen-mast, that is—when a horde of beard weavers swarmed our decks like a herd of weird beavers."

Then the captain's look turned sheepish, and the shrew as it shook turned leapish. "I suppose we weren't *entirely* innocent," he allowed, "as we—after ducking the fog for days—happened to be in the thick of a merry cur hunt. It was off the coast of Afghanistan, where we'd sailed—rigged out like yawl trappers—with a plan to trawl yappers. The crew had been hearing their share about the mutts that lived there: 'If you want to make a killing off sweaters, you should be shearing their hair!'

---

the myopic activist who'd arrived promptly but ineffectually on the shore to hoist a banner reading *SAVE THE WHALE!*

Shauna inhaled a tonic lungful of the enchanted night air, then made her way inside to repose and recuperate on a stuffed piece of furniture designed for comfortable sitting.

At this point, the captain of the docked ship arrived bearing a small furry insectivore as a present, which he set down upon a table that happened to already bear a typically bad-tempered but in this case domesticated mammal of similar features. The captain explained (obviously mistaking Shauna for the occupant of the tower) that, seeing the light and presuming someone was home and awake, he and his fellow sailors had decided to "nop in for a dribble"—having intended, no doubt, to say "drop in for a nibble" (unless perhaps the former phrase is seafaring slang meaning "to stop by for a drink" or "to urinate"—though it seems unlikely that a group of sailors would drop anchor and climb to the top of a lighthouse just to relieve themselves). His crew had followed him up the stairs and now listened raptly to his account of their travels, the purpose of which had been to experience the renowned Japanese cuisine of a certain gauche and virulent Balinese shack known as much for its brawling patrons as for its sublime Alaskan fish fillets. The captain, still drying off from a light rainfall, went on to explain that the voyage

"Well, the shores overflowed with those fashionable curs, and our eyes lit up at their cash-in-able furs. In no time at all our sea-sipping netters had caught a poop-load of the knee-nipping setters. There was no question at all as we looked at our haul that it would be easy to sell sweaters made from these swell setters.

"But as more and more of the burly hounds sprang aboard from our nets with hurly bounds, we discovered that these charmful hoppers had harmful choppers, and soon their darling snouts were giving us snarling doubts. You couldn't step on the poop without being shit in the bins or crapped in the snotch, so it was almost a relief when the Talis came bounding aboard with their warrants and pedigrees and barking tickets and petting fees. They demanded their dog-due in vaunting dictums, portraying themselves as the daunting victims.

"Well, we'd soon had enough of these boring wankers who'd stormed our decks like warring bankers. And so to the sound of shattering barks, accompanied percussively by battering sharks, we shocked our assailants, each soggy dupe, by turning their hounds into doggy soup.

"But the sharks didn't care for such hairy meals, so the dogs got

---

had been interrupted when they were forcibly boarded by government officials off the coast of Afghanistan (an assertion some geographers might find dubious). He claimed they were securing their tertiary mast and quietly attending to their own affairs when a squadron of men with profuse and stylish facial hair thronged aboard like a mutant colony of large Canadian rodents.

As if in recollection of the frightening event, the small furry insectivore trembled and began to jump about, while the captain's look betrayed a guilty conscience as he confessed that he'd neglected to mention one little activity they'd undertaken that might explain the arrival of the local authorities. He recounted how, after a protracted period of inactivity during which they'd drifted in heavy mist, he and his men (there were apparently no women aboard) happened to find themselves on what he called "a merry cur hunt." Though inexperienced at hunting animals over the side of a boat, they were eager to cast their nets and try their luck, having heard that a surefire way to grow rich would be to sell sweaters made from the marvellous hairs of the Afghan hound.

Sure enough, these hounds were so abundant their numbers spilled over into the sea, where they were easily caught. Soon the poop deck was full of the wonderful beasts, and the crew's collective dream of becoming sweater tycoons looked on the verge of coming true.

The only problem was that the big dogs were rather nippy, to the point where

to shore (not even a tail-nip); and though the Talis didn't care for such merry heels, at least we weren't shot to gore (not even a nail-tip). In fact, the weary chintzes, seeing our cheery winces, let us off with a mere rebuke:

"'Listen, you barefaced haggish weirdos,' cautioned one of the hair-faced waggish beardos, 'normally this would mean a sizable jihad not just a mild warning, but we've all had a wild morning: fearful from the blasting (churlish war) and blearful from the fasting (whirlish chore); beset by infidels with knives wagging at us, shouting their spite through shattered teeth (batty frauds), and of course our own wives nagging at us, spouting their shite through tattered sheaths (fatty broads); our prayer mats smell like mare prats; we've got hardly any groom time so our beards are full of tomb grime, and our once-magic tresses are now tragic messes (under all this roiling cotton is a coiling rotten rat's nest where gnats rest—scalp hair that would help scare, for example, the balls off a goat, or the Gauls off a boat); our camels' toes need a tasteful waxing but we can hardly even pay the mortgage on our caves with all the wasteful taxing; plus we're being mocked at by the *Times* and even talked at by the mimes

---

one could hardly step onto the deck without being bit in the shins or snapped in the crotch. Despite their visions of affluence, the captain and his charges were well-nigh relieved when the officials and enforcers boarded their ship with the intention of reclaiming their property. In no uncertain legal terms, these officials demanded the return of the dogs and presented search warrants and identification papers for the missing hounds while issuing fines for disturbing the peace and petting without a permit. A list of rules and transgressions was read with impressive grandiloquence, leaving no question that the victims of this crime would not rest until justice was served. Having had enough of the whole business, the crew began tossing the blasted hounds overboard to the sharks, which had begun thumping against the hull. Only a marine biologist would be qualified to ascertain why the sharks waited till the dogs were safely aboard the vessel before attempting to indulge their appetites for a "curry" lunch. And after all, their portentous swarming might have been in sport, for there's no indication that any of the ejected canines came to harm once back in the heretofore unknown coastal waters of Afghanistan—an outcome the crew (surely?) must have anticipated: i.e., that the sharks wouldn't care for such hirsute victuals, and the dogs, despite the furious barking as they flew from the deck, would merely paddle back to shore unmolested.

At this point, the Afghans could see that there was little hope of getting any

(they say we look like whirligigs in girlie wigs). True, we have silly walks from wearing willy socks but we need those bland socks as sand blocks, for when the sandy devils roar it makes our randy devils sore, and without a slip-slappy foreskin (our preference to doff it is in deference to the Prophet) we're left with flip-flappy sore skin. And as any landlocked sand-socked Quran-cocked desert boy knows—and even salty fops like you faulty sops can understand—a sandy dweller's dandy sweller's worst foe is its first woe: grainy briefs!'

"At the airing of these brainy griefs, the other Tali men—bemoaning such hawkish squalor—burst into a squawkish holler and danced about in their rotting tunics like a band of trotting eunuchs. The mewling drone—baleful noise!—was like the drooling moan of nailful boys. I accosted the one bearable Tali who, in the midst of this terrible ballyhoo, had refrained from the hellish yowling and yellish howling.

"'Look,' said I, 'we don't want to be the proverbial bird in your turbans any more than you want to be the turd in our bourbons. It's a shame to say *cheery ta-ta* in the midst of your teary cha-cha (which, by the way, would make the West End crowds couthlessly rapturous),

---

money out of the trespassing rogues, so they sheathed their pens and prepared to let the seamen off with a warning, though custom would have dictated the waging of a religious war that might ultimately end in the destruction of civilization. After their ostensible leader had delineated the slew of factors contributing to their inclination to relent and free the invaders—ranging from the emotional trauma of living under conditions of perpetual war, through the cognitively diminishing effect of foregoing food for a designated period of time (I surmise the holiday of Ramadan was in full swing); from the anxiety of recurring assaults, physical and verbal respectively, by those who did not share their ideology and by putatively overweight spouses, through the disheartening unhygienic condition of themselves and their belongings (bad enough, we're informed by vivid metaphor, to frighten the testicles off a bearded and horned ungulate); from the taxing financial demands of cave dwelling, through the humiliation of being ridiculed by Western media and pantomime actors for their perambulatory awkwardness (a side-effect of their wearing sand-blocking socks on their penises)—the Afghans became rather wound up and emitted a prolonged and ominous screeching hoot, a bellowing ululation that, in concert with their capering about, evoked impressions of neutered youth injured by multiple spikes.

The captain tried to make peace and facilitate their egress by suggesting that neither party was benefiting from protracting their engagement. To do so, he used

especially after we made you ruthlessly capture us, but I think we'd best be off with a wary *tally-ho* and let you get back to your hairy Tali woe.'

"The noise of the Arabs squawking, those little brutes—like a million scarabs walking on brittle lutes, or a clowder of cats in a rage around a mischief of rats in a cage—only got louder and rose to an ominous pitch, giving me a palminous itch (my sea-stained palms also itch at the sound of pee-stained psalms). It began to remind me of my first wife—easily the worst fife in a band of lobotomized flutists and phlebotomized lutists. What's worse, some of the scabby crooners aboard our crabby schooner were now waving their swords in the lusty feral din, each one a dusty Errol Flynn ready to take on any dense fool in a fence duel.

"Just when it seemed our duck was fried, or at least our goose murdered, the leader of these beard farmers (whom we'd all feared barmers) held forth with a thunderous whistle: instantly the men were silenced, as if a wondrous thistle had been removed from their inner thighs. He looked at me with thinner eyes, reminiscent of one of those linty squids with squinty lids I once tangled with on a journey, and later jangled with on a tourney (beach rugby, that is:

---

a colourful adage, painting images of avian intruders trapped in headdresses, and faeces floating in glasses of straight whisky from Kentucky. In passing, while promoting the idea that best for all concerned would be a swift and amicable departure by the erstwhile dognappers, the captain happened to mention that he thought the ritual song-and-dance routine undertaken by the boarders of his ship would be a smash onstage in London, a town considered by some the world capital in such dramaturgical presentations. As we'll see, this made an unexpectedly strong impression on the mind of the spokesperson for the group. But first, the captain will be off on another of his long-winded discourses.

The noise of the unnerving choir had risen in volume and frequency—with a timbre similar to that of a vast number of dung beetles scritching along the fretted neck of a fragile medieval string instrument liable to splinter at any moment, or a large group of splenetic felines surrounding a confined cluster of sharp-snouted rodents (in technical terms, a "cat ring" around a "rat king," assuming the rodents' tails have become knotted together)—to a degree that occasioned a burning ticklishness in the soft skin on the underside of the captain's hand, and also invoked the first woman he'd married, as she was evidently a terrible performer in a band that could not have been much good to begin with, as it comprised nothing but woodwind players who'd been subject to an operation in which the connections to and from the prefrontal cortex are cut and string players

116

I was in a bonny scrum against some Biscay ruggers when one of those risqué buggers swept in on a hasty tide and latched its fervent suckers onto the tasty hide of my scrawny bum).

"As he took a step toward me, I went into a squat, as if readying for a lopsided scrap—or, just as intimidating, a slop-sided crap. I'd known the art of self-defence since I was a sopping wee urchin with as much brains as a whopping sea urchin. A martial pastor in the Port of Spain (a partial master in the sport of pain) taught me Waikiki kai-wiki, along with some of the more humbling grips— oh, my grumbling hips!—from the *Kama Sutra*, an ancient book of Hindu wrestling holds (in those days nude wrestling and rude nestling were manly ways of instilling in boys, in peerless fashion, a fearless passion for all things masculine).

"In my days of voyaging, I've been taught every art from Tallahassee muscle gashing to Malagasy tussle hashing; from Bora Bora tongue lashing to Tora Bora lung bashing; and from Norman rib-cage mashing to Mormon crib-rage gnashing. My mastery of self-defence is as solid as a delph sea fence. I can as confidently, with the techniques I've acquired, bait a wiggly gobbly gator in Guatemala as

---

who'd one way or another had a considerable amount of blood removed from their bodies. Add to this the fact that the "Talis" (as the captain called them, believing them to be members of an insurgent Islamic fundamentalist political movement that did indeed hold official power for a time, though whether these events take place within that political era or the captain is mistaken in his assumption may never be known) were now brandishing daggers in seeming imitation of a certain swashbuckling film star legendary as much for his "conquests" off-screen as on, and you will not be surprised that the atmosphere was now palpably tense—which is ironic when one considers that the initial impression made by the Afghans when they accosted our seafarers was drably clerical (and perhaps somewhere in that lies a valuable axiom not yet written or otherwise dispensed).

Suddenly the leader of the boarding party silenced his men with a stentorian blast of air through his pursed lips, then narrowed his eyes and gazed at the captain, reminding the latter of certain predatory cephalopods with which he'd been embroiled on more than one occasion. Mistaking this as an inimical gesture, the captain squatted in a manner likely to convey the impression that he was preparing either to trounce his adversary with skillful manoeuvres or defecate in a messy, off-kilter fashion, with either probability being adequate to achieve the goal of making the would-be attacker think twice about skirmishing with him.

The loquacious skipper, at this point in his account, proffered a self-

berate a giggly wobbly waiter in Walla Walla. Other esoteric crafts into which I've been indoctrinated include Bratislavan britch snapping, snotty Bhavan bitch slapping, and—thanks to a Kumbai cabbie in Dubai—Abu Dhabi krabi-kabong and Dabu Abbey crabby-babby bonk. As well, I have attained some degree of adeptness in Jakartan spiral agitation and Spartan gyral decapitation; Philadelphic verbal folly and Delphic Villa fur-ball volley; and, though I'm reluctant to employ either, Gorky tit gripping and Torquay git tripping. I so expertly learned the art of the hurl at fifty-three that I can, for a thrifty fee, stop the heart of an earl with a tainty dart, or even a dainty tart if it has a thick crust and I can get a good kick thrust. Likewise, I've been trained not only to kill two birds with one stone, but to still two Kurds with one bone. When provoked, I am licensed to exercise my prowess in Ouagadougou voodoo and Oaxaca hoodoo-gudu. Then if all else fails and my back's against the wall, I can always aim a trotter and tame any rotter with a series of deft whacks against the balls.

"But after readying myself for a crushing blow, I saw that the scallywag had experienced a mood change: no longer looking quite so much like chewed mange, his face had taken on the aura of a blushing

---

aggrandizing inventory of the international martial arts he'd learned from the time he was a damp, mischievous child with as little sense as a large marine echinoderm to the age of at least fifty-three (when he supposedly learned to assassinate noblemen with small poisoned projectiles and, in a pinch, delicate little pastries with delectable fillings). His dubious introduction to these athletics was at the hands of a pugnacious Christian minister who taught him what were supposedly "wrestling holds" from a time-worn Sanskrit tome meant, in actuality, to instruct the more erotically enthralled in advanced lovemaking techniques. At the conclusion of delineating his vast résumé of combative aptitudes, the captain indicated that should his more exotic tactics come up short, he could always resort to expertly kicking his opponent in the scrotum.

Finally, however, it dawned on the captain that the Afghan gent's posture and expression were not bellicose but rather shy and inquisitive—that he had, so it seemed, assumed the countenance of a glossy black bird whose cheeks were flushing pink with embarrassment (though invisibly so, given the veil of feathers). The truth is, the captain would have done better all along to appeal to this man's vanity than to intimidate him with a warlike, or dangerously incontinent, pose. Had he known that the secret dream of this fellow and his charges was to make their mark on the theatrical stage rather than in the theatre of war, he might have done just that.

crow. He gazed up at me with a look both searching and lost, like a bashful heron, or a hash-full baron who was both lurching and sauced.

"'Do you really think we're ready for the stage?' he asked.

"'Ready for the stage?' I repeated in a geekish, galing, glazy, gauzy echo, sounding for all the world, I'm sure, like nothing quite so much as an eekish, ailing, lazy, Ozzie gecko. 'Ready for the stage!' I said again, but this time more in the tone of a carny bloke on blarney coke. 'With the right *mise* for your *scène*, and seas for your men'—few survive the voyage from that land where even the most cocky roast, to that far rocky coast beyond which lie the rolly hills and holy rills of Britain the Great (as for dropping in by plane, unless they could pass themselves off as British scholars, these skittish brawlers would stand a better chance plopping in by drain)—'not only,' I shat them, 'are you ready for the stage but crowds will be steady for the rage of the season: a grumpy old feel-good Rama-drama at the frumpy old Gielgud Dramarama! Put a Berkeley chorus with your choir, so you don't quirkily bore us with your ire, and you'll have queues stretching in twenty-two aisles'— and later retching in twenty-two styles—'between all the stylish bars full of bile-ish stars and every weary dress den in the dreary West

---

When asked if he thought they were "ready for the stage," the skipper was initially dumbfounded, making sounds and expressions common to a particular species of Australian lizard. He quickly regained himself, though, when he divined the opportunity to humour his opponent and make an escape. Switching his tone to that of a sideshow huckster high on a type of illicit drug (favoured by psychoanalytic geniuses and high-living lowlifes) with the propensity to foster a gift for flattering deception, the captain proceeded to concoct a scenario in which the howling desert rubes would become without question the darlings of Western high culture, singing and dancing their way on the London stage to untold popular and critical acclaim. To his credit, and good fortune, the captain was well versed in the theatrical lifestyle. It's not known to us quite how this came to be, but clearly the old salty dog knew the ins and outs of thespian stagecraft and lore like a Gielgud—the structural namesake of whom would be, in this deceptive cajoling, the venue of the Talis's great footlight-bathed success. Just as fortunate, and equally peculiar, is that this Afghan troupe should happen to be admirers of the iconic terpsichorean director whose name the captain cited as a stylistic paragon. On the other hand, they could not accept the inspired vision of the captain— who seemed almost to believe he might make his whole fanciful confabulation a reality—that the production contain, if you'll excuse my using his own bawdy phraseology, "tits." (Assuming the captain was correct in his political identification

End: a twittering glitz of glittering twits! Every nitwit Brit-crit lit-snit pundit git will have a shit-fit! *This ditzy blitz with its fit-writ skits has wit, grit, ritz, and tits!* they'll spit in inky flares from their finky lairs. From the woollish cliffs of Dover, with their dullish whiffs of clover, to snoring Wales, with its warring snails that battle all the way to Cornwall, a worn call will be heard: *Hit show!* (Though if I were a critic I'm sure I'd climb the nearest crow's nest, raise my nose crest, and yell at the top of my lung—I lost the other in a vulgar bet to a Bulgar vet—with the lop of my tongue—it was once nipped by a cussy parrot who mistook it for a pus-y carrot: *Shit-ho!*)

"'We are Busby Burka fans,' said the guy from the Tali, 'but we can't have any of those trashy bits with brashy—'

"I cut him off like a Thai from the galley who'd just beheaded a clattering beaver with a battering cleaver: 'There will be no tasteless parts—it'll all be as clean as paste-less tarts! For the theme-y song, the, uh, Buzz Burka Chorines will simply take their sheets and drop them phlegmatically, then shake their teats and flop them dramatically. Beneath those blanky-cloaks, which make them look like clanky blokes, they'll wear just nipple stickers and stipple

---

of this delegation, they would be wont to participate in any endeavour that did not adhere to the strict tenets of Sharia law—which, mind you, may have overlooked such a contingency.) When he explained, however, that it would all be in good taste and that the chorus girls would simply remove their burkas and wiggle their breasts in a manner consistent with the overarching dramatics of the show, they had no problem with that—or even, it seems, with the captain's insistence that their staging be laden enough with such tropes to make even the flaccid member of an ascetic Himalayan holy man powerfully erect.

Some personal information about the captain that emerged during this latest spell of jabbering is that he forfeited a lung in a wager to a Slavic veteran of war and that part of his tongue had been cropped by the beak of a tropical bird who thought it was a purulent but nonetheless palatable root vegetable.

Having then consulted the captain on the matter of hiring a renowned composer and a noted choreographer (unconcerned by their evidently Judaic descent despite the cultural and religious differences—an instance, perhaps, of art transcending partisanship and discrimination), the Afghan spokesman turned to his men for their assent. This time their raucous hooting was of a delighted, affirmative nature, yet startling and grating enough to upset the captain's stomach (problems with which we'll hear more of later). Yet it did not deter him from distending his ruse by giving to the chief Talib the business card of a charlatan

knickers, or a seamy thong. The sight of our loopy drama's riff-raff staging should set even a droopy lama's stiff staff raging!'

"'That is acceptable, but one more thing.' His plumpish partisan eyes were now as wide as lumpish artisan pies. 'Do you think we could get Harvey Gershwinstein to fluff up the score with some gripping tunes?'

"'Not only will we get Harvey Gershwinstein to write some dotty wrenchers,' I lied through my rotty dentures, 'but we'll get Garvey Hirschwinstein to choreograph some steps so you won't just scuff up the floor like tripping goons.'

"His face was now blushing so flaringly and flushing so blaringly it looked as if he had frozen cheeks. He turned to his chosen freaks to see what they thought of these trusty goals. As one, the gusty trolls let loose another barking howl, which set my harking bowel a-tumble groan-ally (unless it was the yeast of the beer—a kitschy brew called Beast of the Year, much loved by my normally bitchy crew—which set it a-grumble tonally).

"Now that these hairy folks had fallen for my fairy hoax, it was time to reel in the impish wankers, along with our wimpish anchors.

---

who once sold "schmaltz" and now sells "grist for mills," concerning whom a new oratory would be inaugurated. Frankly, I'd just as soon not go into much detail about the bogus merits of this "Grady Shea" and his sidekick "One-Prick Tony" (surname Bird), for I find myself mildly appalled that the captain would take his joke this far even on what might be a band of scoundrels, and also because I'm getting a bit bored by now with the captain's long-windedness (as you'll see, I'm not the only one). I will nevertheless relay that these two con artists were to be the supposed experts who would take the budding stars from day one of rehearsals through opening night in the prestigious West End. And I should mention as well that one element of the monologue (though not to the exclusion of others) makes me wonder if it's the captain's wry hoodwinking or nascent senility that's getting the best of him when he speaks of essential training in "deboning" a codpiece. Being a sailor, can he not think of the preparation of a "cod" without the necessity of filleting? Is it his way to poke fun by a sort of quaint wordplay at the enthusiasm of his dupes, implying that they will need a savvy tutor to diminish their erections before they can put on their stage attire? Is there, unbeknownst to me, a traditional model of codpiece that's fluffed out by ribbing that must be removed before donning? Or is this a flub indicative of the onset of aphasia, the dawning of a cognitive decline? My suspicion is that it's most of the above, but that the captain's linguistic falterings have long been a part of his

I proffered the card of one Lean-Eyed Grady, a bony fraud and phony broad (alias the Green-Eyed Lady) who used to make his living selling schmaltz and smelling-salts but now scams a lot of dollars (and thereby damns a lot of scholars) selling grist for mills and, in the off-season, mist for grills. The guy was a walking chancre, a real shocking wanker (speaking of such) who wouldn't know *The Taming of the Shrew* from *The Shaming of the True*: in short, a most incriminating and destructive gent with a complexion of shady grey.

"'The moment you dock in Kent, find a call box and phone Grady Shea—a most discriminating and instructive gent. No one-trick pony, Grady and his esteemed colleague, One-Prick Tony, will assist you and your troupe with every challenge along the way—from first rehearsals at Lurie Drain in crafty Dorset, through opening night at Drury Lane in drafty corsets. Whatever might be giving you a bother—be it the speaking of lines or the leaking of spines—Grady Shea and Tony Bird will be there to solve it. They'll instruct you on everything from how to fall through trap doors wearing tap drawers, to how to sip chalet booze in ballet shoes. You'll learn how to debone a codpiece and de-cone a bod-piece, as well as, for

---

makeup, and should not occasion too much concern on our part.

I had intimated that at least one other would find the captain's verbosity boring, and now I will explain. The commander's own navigator had fallen asleep in the midst of his tale and was snoring interruptively in a way that might be mistaken for the rhythmic expulsion and sucking-in of air through vulvar labia but with overtones evocative of a manual tool fitted with a spindle-like metal rod penetrating deeper and deeper into blood-spurting flesh, or a crying lovelorn ground-dwelling monkey of the callositously crimson-bottomed variety so sexually aroused it carries on the act of coitus even in the absence of its long-absquatulated object of desire. In other words, by my lay diagnosis, the sound of a lasciviously salivary casualty of sleep apnea with concomitant chronic sinus congestion—a condition I would wish on no one, least of all a gentle soul trying to sleep in the next room or same bed as the afflicted, though it did in this case have the boon of stopping the captain mid-sentence and subsequently hastening the conclusion of his speech.

The first mate explained in an aside to Shauna that such garrulousness had earned his captain the sobriquet "Rant-Away Jack," while the boatswain sought an end to the navigator's snoring by stuffing a crumpled cartographic broadside into his mouth—a stratagem that worked without, somehow, waking the sleeper.

With the navigator no longer sounding like a dunce with tracheal inflammation

example, how to shush a heckler and hush a shekel-er. Under their expert tutelage you'll discover the secrets of attaining lewd jaws like Jude Laws, or even getting into dames' jeans like James Deans. If you need advice on how you should deal with your fame, or even feel with your dame, G and T will be there. Suffering from paralyzing stage fright, or perhaps even sterilizing page fright? G 'n' T will help you overcome your nerves with their patented spined bells that bind spells and overnumb your curves. Painful jowls? Those joggling bells—along with a combination of T 'n' G's proprietary boggling gels—will have you up singing and dancing in no time, like a bunch of Janeful Powells. You'll be pouring your hearts out to—'"

Before he could finish recounting this quackish briefing, the captain was interrupted by a brackish queefing—a sound both squalorous-and-dirty and dolorous-and-squirty, like a hand drill in meat that's still got a pumping heart, or a mandrill in heat that's still got a humping part but is all alone, the rude lecher, and weeping sleazily. The sound, however, was from no such lewd retcher, nor was it from ladies' groins or a baboon's—or even the aforementioned Grady's—loins (speaking of man-drills). It was

---

atop an uncastrated male horse or slobbering female tiger, the captain drew the present segment of his bloated anecdote to a close by noting that the Afghans, content with the particulars of this strange man from the United Kingdom's scheme to make them stage sensations, or so stultified by his elaborately detailed proposal that they were happy to let on so, slipped their swords back into their scabbards and got back into their little boat—though one of them, having been mistaken earlier for one of the curs and thrown overboard, was already swimming behind the landward fleet of pooches, looking for all the world like a dandified mermaid.

Taking from his metallic hat an intricate feather and making rhythmic yet disjointed movements, the captain paused in his narrative to reflect on the philosophical exhortation he'd given his men as they resumed their voyage to Bali. He quoted his own lofty and sentimental speech about the majesty and spiritual significance of the sea quest that lay ahead.

The crew, who were increasingly hungry and wanted his tedious reminiscence to reach its conclusion so they might be fed, managed to snap him out of his romantic digression by reminding him of the next dramatic misadventure they'd suffered on their trip: a storm that blew them off course and left them drifting at sea with little in the way of food to sustain them. It seems the journey was going so smoothly they'd started to enjoy themselves a little too much. During

simply that the navigator had dozed off and was sleeping wheezily.

"Man overboard!" called the bosun, referring to either the antique captain and the antics of his manic anticlimactic anecdote, or his "overbored" helmsman who'd fallen from the ship of waking and was now, with a sinner's ease, at the mercy of the whip of shaking inner seas.

"We don't call him Rant-Away Jack for nothing," noted the first mate to Shauna, who all this time had been listening gamely, though not without glistening lamely, to the captain's wearisome tale. "Our dear captain," he continued, "will babble on and hyper-bore ya from Babylon to Hyperborea."

The bosun scrunched up a map from which he'd munched up a scrap ("Be wary of print that leaches and lint that preaches!" was the oft-remembered avuncular advice of his carbuncular uncle Av Arbuckle), then approached the navigator and stuffed the map in his craw. The crap in his maw did not rouse the lousy dreamer, who slept on like a drowsy lemur, but he no longer made the noises one might tend to associate with a croupy dolt on a droopy colt or drooly tigress.

"But I truly digress," admitted the captain, who then attempted

---

afternoon tea they became inebriated to such a degree they steered right into the tempest and were tossed helplessly around by the ferocity of its winds. When the seas settled, they found nothing left in their stores but a pot roast that was well past its prime—to the extent that, as the captain reflected bizarrely, it was about as gastronomically tempting as a cooked child. Still, they minced it into a sort of ground beef and managed to get it down, with possibly detrimental effects on their brains and teeth. The youngest of the sailors were particularly appalled, recounted the captain, but the others had laughed as they gagged and made humorous statements to the effect that it was really quite a delightful meal—just like sitting in the Pagan Stork pub back home and eating a succulent dish made of pig and deer.

One of the crew interjected to state acerbically that it had been more akin to sitting in the Olde Foggy Dude and noshing a type of canned mush concocted in a factory to meet the basic nutritional requirements and culinary demands of a housebound cur.

The lighthouse erupted in laughter, and one can imagine even Shauna and the sentry, if he were to overhear from his post, having a good chuckle at the witticism.

Their hysterics were cut short by the appearance of Ronna, a lovely young woman who'd been hired to do light housekeeping (a sort of mer-maid, so to speak), assist with office work, and care for the sick animals taken in by the

to wrap up his tale like a Captain Ahab trying to trap up his whale (no dopy mick, he'd read every word of *Mopy Dick*—except the ones that might be found offensive to a gentleman half-Irish and half-English such as himself). "So anyway, everybody in the sandy horde sheathed his handy sword, with its shiny tip, and went back to their tiny ship—except for one lone bugger who'd already swum for shore, like a foppish mermaid, in the wake the dogs' moppish fur made (mistaken for a hound, he'd been thrown from the boat like a bone from the throat of, as the first mate put it, 'a limey hick getting a Heimy-lick')."

The captain took from his tin cap an articulated plume and began to gesture like a particulated loom. "Now free of yowly beasts and bowelly yeasts, free of debt peelers and pet dealers (who'd guarded their hairy wares like wary hares), it was time, as I said to my trusty carousers, to once again heal your soul and brave the seas!"

"Oh, seal your hole and save the breeze," muttered one of the crew. "I'm hungry."

"It was time," the quilled skipper waxed on, "to venture sanely with virgin sails upon the sea's vaulted sermon, time to censure vainly

---

master of the lighthouse. One could be excused for wondering if Ronna's fair appearance factored into her attaining this new position, for her previous work experience consisted primarily of evangelizing about the Christian Messiah and setting cheese on fire (though, to be fair, she had achieved considerable renown in that latter pursuit—especially at one locale in Japan, where her virtuosic torching of Greek cheese annually took top prize). I do not mean to diminish or otherwise disparage the cheesemaker's art—for Ronna, beyond torching such dairy products, did herself make a wide variety of pressed and in some cases fermented milk curds—it's just that a direct relation of that craft to veterinary and zoological care, secretarial tasks, and high-altitude domestic maintenance is hardly conspicuous. And yet she did have a winning personality and would give any prospective employer a first impression of smarts and dedication. Perhaps the lighthouse keeper also detected a quality of forbearance, which he knew, with what little self-awareness he possessed, would be essential in anyone working closely under him. But we're getting ahead of ourselves. The important things to know about Ronna at this point—to the extent that any of this can with certitude be catalogued as important—are that she executed her present duties well, that she made an impressive array of cheeses, from Abbot's Gold to Zanetti (drawing the line only at ones she considered immoral), and that notwithstanding her virtuous nature and strictly observed chastity, she did have something of a coquettish streak

with surgeon veils upon the sea's salted vermin, time to—"

"Avast! Spare us the soppy cheese!" bellowed the newly woken navigator, a skilled quipper, "and get to the part with the choppy seas!"

The captain, in a momentary goutful daze, looked about with a doubtful gaze. Then, with the flourish of a magician pulling a rabbit out of a hat, or a behaviourist pulling a habit out of a rat, he came to his senses and skipped ahead in his tale.

"Right—the tempest! Well, after the cunning plan of our punning clan had failed, we set sail again and were on our way to Bali dutifully, but the voyage was going so well we began to dally beautifully. In fact, we got so sauced at tea we meandered into a storm and got tossed at sea. We were flung about by those rig-ripping waters like a delirious gang of wig-whipping rotters. Worst of all, there was nothing left to eat but some leftover meat: a potted roast that looked like a rotted post. Well, that toasted rot was about as appetizing as a roasted tot, I can tell you. And though less awful when minced, still my men winced as they sat in bound grief and ate the ground beef. Drowning this ghoul—that is, downing this gruel—didn't do much for our mental dispositions, nor, for that

---

that could sometimes draw unwelcome advances from, for example, hypocritical clergymen. She was, however, more than capable of handling herself.

Ronna set down on the coffee table, next to the small furry mammals, a dish of the cheeses for which she was known and a thick strand of delectable hard buttery candy that softens when chewed (perhaps not the wisest choice of dessert for a bunch of scurvy dogs whose dental condition was fragile at best).

"Please chatter!" encouraged Ronna, but an uncomfortable silence prevailed, for this otherwise charming maiden (proselytizing aside) had spent so much time in the company of pungent cheeses and ripe animals that her rank aura left the room speechless.

The captain, ignorant of the source of this fetor or perhaps just oblivious to decorum, broke the silence by asking, "Does anyone smell socks?" Noticing that Ronna blushed at this question, the captain backtracked and pretended he'd made a slip of the tongue and had actually meant to ask if there were any merchants of loose protective overalls among them, claiming unconvincingly that he needed such a garment for a lecture he intended to deliver on the subject of whether or not fire drills were crucial but insignificant exercises.

The social awkwardness of the moment was boisterously dispelled by an eager pig who dashed into the room and began guzzling wine, which had evidently been set out in glasses at a low altitude for guests (though a bottle unattended

matter, our dental mispositions (you'd need a steel mandible to make that meal standable). The newest members of our crew found this rare hazing somewhat hair-raising, but the rest of us cheerfully joked as we jeerfully choked that it was just like eating stag 'n' pork at the Pagan Stork."

"More like eating old doggy food at the Olde Foggy Dude," observed a crewman.

The ensuing laughter was interrupted by the appearance of the fetching Ronna, recently employed by the lighthouse keeper (presently off visiting his cousin, the kitehouse leaper) to do light housekeeping, act as secretary, and tend to the retching fauna (though, given the size of the ailing menagerie, she spent more time wiping up turds than typing up words). Much admired for both her vestal chastity and chestal vastity, Ronna had spent her life chittering about Jesus while—for this "purdy creature" was also a curdy preacher—jittering about cheeses. A chic-ish reverend of reekish Chevre and a true minister of Munster, Ronna could make a Roquefort that would make folk roar, and everyone from woozy bailors to boozy whalers were known to densely wail for her Wensleydale. One could hardly

---

might be successfully suckled by one of these canny creatures, so that should not be discounted as an alternate or additional means by which the guzzling occurred).

The first mate mistook the pig for a white rhinoceros and commented, with some degree of awe, that it was quite an alcoholic. The boatswain corrected him, saying it was just a perspiring swine enjoying a little quaff. Then the navigator chimed in, making the rather startling admission that, regardless of what type of animal it was, the sight of its bald hindquarters was giving him serious thoughts of bestiality as a means to end his unbidden celibacy.

Just as he was about to wager that the sow was game for sexual intercourse, a cry of pain pierced the air: Ronna had lost her step and fallen on a novelty telephone in the shape of a rabbit, striking her ulnar nerve in the process. She had no idea what had happened, and the first thing that crossed her mind was that a pyromaniac must have somehow fractured her arm near the elbow—perhaps a Freudian assumption best left to the experts, or perhaps just a recognition that she herself (a "pyro" of cheese) was responsible for the accident. In any case, she immediately picked up the receiver and tearfully bellowed her account of the incident to her chiropractor.

With a mind to take her thoughts off the pain and perhaps even bring her a snicker or two, the captain—clearly suffering, or enjoying, the effects of age-related cognitive deterioration—simulated a spoken dispute with a drunken sea creature

blame fools for falling in love with this geeky cheeser when they saw her flame boules and other frilly cheeses (her Saganaki—first prize each year at Nagasaki—could melt any heart's chilly freezes). Indeed, as many stinking bishops have tried to make her as she's made Stinking Bishops, but she'll have no such cheeky geezer. Long ago this maker of chalky cheeses vowed that if she were just another cartless horse on life's heartless course, the only one who'd ride her was her jockey Jesus. Yea, though our swanky miss is holier than manky Swiss, she still has a dash of flirtiness (but never with a flash of dirtiness!) and her drives are leery enough that's she's careful around men whose lives are dreary enough or who show signs of crude lust— those cheery losers who are not so chaste in teases and have no taste in cheeses. As for her own taste in cheeses, Ronna can be a leery chooser: she often made Abbot, for example, but never Blue Castello (the "lewd crust" put her off).

Placing upon the coffee table a toffee cable and a cheese platter, she encouraged the suddenly quiet guests to "Please chatter!"

The stooping wench emitted such a whooping stench, the captain couldn't help but ask, "Does anyone smell socks—er, I

---

sometimes mistaken for a lady adapted to the marine realm. Some of those present felt that his histrionics had grown excessive when he began viciously berating the poor aquatic beast. When the concocted discussion ended at last—the pardonable beast had succumbed to the captain's base vanity and suspended the pursuit of its point of view—the lamentable Irishman (who was, in fact, as I mentioned, half English) performed an act of legerdemain by extracting a marsupial insectivore native to Australia and New Guinea from a boot-shaped confection. So far nothing was working, for despite his doting foolery Ronna continued to weep. His next tack—perhaps a little desperate and juvenile for a man of his years—was to try to elicit a giggle by jabbing at her ribcage with a billiards stick he'd crafted from a splendid wooden bench once reserved for lower primates at a certain temple where agents of prostitutes worshipped. Seeing that even this effort failed to draw a smile, the captain, that predicament-solving obtainer of cargo, decided it was time to pull out all the stops with his ever-popular consciousness-altering one-man silent theatrical production of a rather objectionable comedic piece about a snobbish and sad lady of the night and a spotted door riddled with perforations. Well, that silent thespian of an old seafarer figuratively removed the soft, layered rocks that were weighing him down and vigorously wiggled his bottom, adroitly parading his dilapidated antique body like a horny, slovenly, burlesque-dancing, geriatric matron. While this little show, true to the tradition of pantomime,

mean," seeing that his reference to the cheddar reek had given her a redder cheek, "sell smocks? I need a tall smock for a small talk I plan to give on the subject of…of…The Fire Drill: Is It But a Dire Frill?"

Recoiling from the cheesy air, Shauna sank a little deeper into her easy chair.

At that moment, a willing swine darted in and started swilling wine.

"That white rhino is a right wino," commented the first mate.

"It's not a rhino," corrected the bosun, "just a sweaty pig having a petty swig."

"I don't care if it's a groundhog drinking hound grog," confessed the navigator, who was also the sail mender and the mail sender. "My male state has been in such a stalemate that that critter's hairless butt is starting to look as inviting as a bearless hut on a stormy night. I'll bet you four bucks that boar—"

A shriek from across the room rent the air: Ronna had tripped and smacked her funny bone on the novelty bunny phone. A moment after falling on the bone, she was bawling on the phone to her chiropractor, wailing that some pyro cracked her (though

---

employed no verbal expression, it still had its pronounced sonic aspect, owing to a gastrointestinal condition that flared up at the most inconvenient times— one understood in the past to be the exclusive property of a worm-ridden rotund herbivore with a prehensile proboscis, and quite foreign to sea captains.

"That's a class act," murmured a previously unnoted member of the crew with regard to the captain's percussively flatulent disruption of his own determinedly silent antics. To make matters worse, the act's most deftly articulated theme— the speckled door full of holes—was disgracefully demolished by the bum of the pig who, after finishing off the wine and cheese, tottered backwards through the imaginary structure like a male deer suffering from nervous clumsiness.

A member of the audience—a crew member, I should say—shattered the silence by asking tactlessly if there mightn't be a hot beverage to follow their light repast, of which he partook little owing to the gusto of the pig on its epicurean rampage. He stated with facetious hyperbole that, failing coffee and a supplementary serving of cheese, he would be content with a wrinkled plum covered in ashy powder and a small coffin full of avian carcasses—which could, in seriousness, be construed as a basket of chicken tenders, but I think he was just being ridiculous.

At that point the captain, who seemed to take life very lightly and art very seriously, went berserk, tearing at his shirt and emitting what could perhaps best

seeing there was no flame on the bone, she should surely have put the blame on the phone).

To cheer her up, the captain, in his matured sanity, pretended he was arguing with a saturated manatee. This talking charade soon became a shocking tirade, for the sea beast would not be ceased. His mock chat finally over—the venial manatee having given in to his menial vanity—the tragic mick did a magic trick and produced a bandicoot from a candy boot, but still Ronna sobbed. Next, the shining wit tried to amuse her by poking her ribs with a pool cue he'd carved from a cool pew that had once been the perch for chimps at the Church for Pimps. Still no laughter, so it was time for that bind-mending stow-shopper to bring down the lighthouse with his mind-bending show-stopper—a mime routine called The Haughty Doleful Whore Behind the Dotty Holeful Door. Well, that mime of an ancient mariner took out his shale and shook out his tail, rippingly strutting his dumpy old frame like a strippingly rutting frumpy old dame. But while phonically silent, this pantomime was still sonically violent, for the captain was prone to a condition he called "the terminal vapours"—a disorder previously thought to affect only verminal tapirs.

---

be described as a "mirth bark"—the sort of irrational and complex bellow typically heard only in times of celebratory debauchery. In doing so, he exposed a splotch on his chest—a bit of God's own graffiti in the shape of a manta or "devil" ray. He began to snap his jaws and blather, raving incantatorially as he stomped about the room in pursuit of the pig. The more the pig eluded him, the more his men seemed to enjoy the show. When he finally caught his porcine prey, he landed on it with a force seemingly as great as a falling cabin and some large rocks.

The situation was worse than it looked for both the captain and the pig because Ronna, trying to get out of her painful funk, had begun mopping the floor with a bed rag—and that was the very spot where the two went down. The surface was so slippery with suds that they slid right out of the room, under the guardrail and out into mid-air, where they appeared momentarily frozen in suspended animation, like the photographic image of two loggers battling in a luminous mist. The sound that swiftly succeeded their descent was horrible to the ears: a nauseating double thump that left Ronna in stunned supplication to her god and Shauna in serious disequilibrium, her complexion the colour of aluminum that has undergone replication by means of a digital imaging device. Speechless, she swooned toward the sea and dropped at the feet of the boatswain, who was anxiously looking for his dear captain in the direction from which the wind was blowing. The small furry insectivore leapt about with evident distress, perhaps

"That's a class act," muttered one of his crew as the captain's ass clacked.

The spunky schoonerist soldiered on—a bold hack who couldn't hold back—but no artful factor of the ailing farce could redeem this fartful actor of the failing arse. A further disgrace finally ended the show when its most artistically constructed illusion—the barrier of the door—was vulgarly shattered by the derrière of the boar, who, with the grim panache of a drowning bee, had imbibed every drop of the prim Grenache (and the Bordeaux) while greedily downing Brie, and now staggered backwards through the invisible partition like a fumbling buck.

The silence that followed was broken by another of the crewmen: "Um...the Kanduri toffee and the Camarillo tamarillo and other fruitish bits all looked good, but that foxy pig ate every last poxy fig. I don't suppose I could get just a tandoori coffee and a basket of curds? My stomach is having such brutish fits, if I don't eat something pretty soon I'll settle for a sooty prune and a casket of birds."

The captain—who'd sooner be mutinied than upstaged (to feel a lot of spite, just steal his spot of light)—was dreaming of dusting

---

picking up in some subtle way best defined and articulated by specialists in animal behaviour the funereal sadness of the crew as they morbidly sobbed at the surely fatal mishap that had befallen their leader.

The boatswain, with a look in his eyes as if they'd been selected from a package of frozen bovine orbs in a supermarket meat bin, hailed him as a god of the oceans, a Neptune. The sentry bayed like a rueful doofus and, by way of honouring the pig and the captain, blasted a round of ammunition out to sea. He mistakenly (though, under the circumstances, rather aptly) referred to the fallen skipper as Captain Ineptune. Had the captain been an incompetent singer who couldn't carry a tune, and had the sentry and others been forced to hear the spew of such a crooner, perhaps a name like that would have served as a fond tribute to a "king of seas" who could only "sing off keys"! But I've gone off on a tangent. The significant thing about the marksman's gesture is that he happened to shoot a passing albatross—an ominous act from both a literary and ethical perspective.

In response to the sentry's odd toast, Shauna half-rose from the floor to offer a nauseous hurrah. Then Ronna stopped praying upon the sudden realization that she had no idea of the identity of the man for whose safety or soul she was petitioning. Who, she asked (rather in the vein of a fundamentalist theatre critic) was that "cheesy queer"?

Ignoring the epithet—which was, after all, ambiguous and not necessarily

down the boar for busting down the door. Uttering a sort of revel-day mirth bark, he tore at his shirt, exposing a devil-ray birthmark. Then he chomped as he ranted and he romped as he chanted, charging at the boar for barging at the door. The jerky pig attempted to elude him with a kind of perky jig. (Always happy to bet on both fun and war, the crew placed odds of one and four.)

For the willful skipper, chasing the pig (a skillful whipper) was like trying to catch a greyhound in a hayground. But after a fair run—which his men thought rare fun—he actually managed to fell the sucker.

The beast went down as if a shack and boulders had fallen on its back and shoulders—but it didn't stop, for it had landed on the very spot where Ronna, still moping and sopping, had taken a bed rag from a red bag and begun soaping and mopping the floor. The pig and the captain slid on the thickening suds, flew from the room and under the rail, hovered fleetingly in the fog light like a couple of lumberjacks in a log fight, then plummeted—with sickening thuds—to the ground far below.

Ronna, shocked, began to pray while Shauna rocked and began

---

pejorative—the first mate launched into a pointlessly convoluted account of how the captain—christened Ray by his parents—came to be known as Jack. Before he could get very far, a painful yelp (sounding much like a piratical greeting, and nearly a phonetic reversal of the captain's original name) drowned him out. The yelp, of course, belonged to none other than the captain—up from his fall and in from a fresh downpour, battered and bleeding but obviously very much alive.

The seamen were ecstatic at the sight of their leader, and true to form the small furry insectivore twirled with apparent delight.

The navigator asked the question on everyone's mind: how did the captain survive his dire tumble?

The answer to that question can be explained by a combination of chaos theory, synchronicity conjecture, and Fortean philosophy: sensitive dependence on initial conditions combined with an acausal connecting principle and a textbook example of the damnedest thing happening. Had the pig not gorged itself on cheese and wine (especially the rich Boursin and heavy Bordeaux), it might not have attained the essential suppleness and girth to provide such a non-aerodynamic cushion for the captain who, fortuitously, was falling directly above it, and if not for the singular occurrence of a giant squid washing up onshore on that very spot where they were about to fall, the pig would almost certainly have been fatally wounded. So it was a confluence of factors in an improbable sequence

to sway, her tanned skin suddenly pale as scanned tin. Glazed and dumb and lurching seaward, she fell at the feet of the bosun, dazed and glum and searching leeward. The shrew leapt worriedly as the crew wept luridly, certain their captain would voyage no more.

"He was a king of the seas—a real Neptune," sobbed the fraught bosun, with a look in his eyes like they'd been bought frozen.

Then the sentry howled like a sorry galoot and fired off a round in a gory salute (he shot an albatross gliding nearby). "To Captain Ineptune and his flying pig!" the poor sinner brayed outside the doorway where Ronna, the Boursiner, prayed.

Shauna half-rose with a queasy cheer, then Ronna—still propped in her stare—stopped in her prayer to ask, of no one in particular, "Who was that cheesy queer?"

The first mate turned to Ronna, that sizzler of cheese, and spoke of his captain, that chiseller of seas: "He was born with the mark of a beast called the manta, so his parents named him Ray, but to all those who knew him, and some who did not, he was simply known as—"

"Yar!" came a yelp of roaring pain, as a figure stepped in from the pouring rain.

---

that saved the two—a matter of, as pious observers such as Ronna might have it, the Lord working in strange and mysterious ways. Which is not to say their landing was entirely cushy: Nature and Chance had done what they could to make their meeting with the earth relatively comfortable; however, humanity had erected a concrete wall to lessen the force of wave against shore, and it was into this rampart that the pig and sailor thudded after sliding from the back of the slippery kraken.

The fall seemed to have further disintegrated the captain's personality: one moment the English half of his character would dominate and he'd describe his pain by the use of a British slang term denoting surprise and alarm, the next his Irish half would take over and he'd attempt to convey the intensity of his impact with the wall in an analogy referencing an Irish post-mortem ritual.

The captain had just finished relating the essentials of his fall and rise when the keeper of the lighthouse returned, soaking wet and in a foul mood. Mr. Albert Ross—and it seems no one commented on the curious fact that one albatross would plummet moments before another "albertross" would rise—was back from his cousin's kitehouse (I confess ignorance of that form of structure) where he'd found quarters unexpectedly cramped: his kindly cousin had offered lodgings to the crew of a ship that had snagged on rocks and sunk just after leaving harbour, along with a disreputable and dangerous chap of advanced years who'd been causing a ruckus at the local taproom. It was on those same premises that, while

"—Jack!"

The sailors burst with joy, for the old bleeder who stood before them was none other than their bold leader.

"But, Captain, how did you survive that drastic spill?" asked the navigator, as the shrew twirled about like a spastic drill.

"Well, as I looked down I saw that pig billow in its fall—so full of Boarsin and Boardeaux it made a nice big pillow (one size fits all). The downward spin scared me but the pig's skin spared me. So I'm saved, but—" (here the captain, part limey boor, paused for effect) "—*blimey*—sore!"

"Praise the Lord," said Ronna, "but what about our slimy boar?"

"Oh, his crumbling bacon was saved by a bumbling kraken that washed up on shore. He slid from that squid like a mail truck on trail muck and we both hit the breakwall with all the force of a wake brawl—hence the thud and the blood."

Just then the keeper of the tower—a Mr. Albert Ross—flew in, soaked from the fetid weather and looking much like a tattered bird with wetted feather.

He was back from the abode of his cousin Drew who was

---

making his way home at the conclusion of the familial visit, our lighthouse keeper downed upward of twenty drinks (for which one can hardly blame him, given the unpleasant necessity of having had to share a narrow sleeping berth with more than a dozen coarse men). An amusing side tale about the young Ethiopian woman who was serving him his saltwater whiskies: she was a madcap fibber who insisted she had two hearts and had committed smutty acts on film with a massive hairy land mammal of fearsome aspect. And yet, why shouldn't such claims be true!

Drink can cause a man to do things the scope of his normal tendencies would not predict. On a perverse whim, the lighthouse keeper added a further intoxicant to the one he was imbibing, then, in the fashion of a certain Romantic poet whose cultivated entrancements bred sublime verse, gave motion to a dapper feather pen and commenced an ode to the Abyssinian maid. But like the voyage · of his bunkmates who'd barely set sail before fortune intervened and put an end to the enterprise, no sooner had his dreamily opiated authorship been launched than it was interrupted by a man from Porlock. The stunning appearance of the interloper—a milksop garbed in the tawdry and eerie glamour of a sex-trade sorcerer—disturbed the lighthouse keeper's mystic enthrallment and triggered in him a fit of drooling and shrieking.

This drew the professional curiosity of two psychiatrists recognized for both their work in curing patients of sexual guilt and their adroitness at shucking oysters

billeting a dozen crew from a ship that had (soon after it was boarded) sunk and with whom our lighthouse codger, as kitehouse lodger, was forced to share a sordid bunk—in company with a creaky old loser they'd found waving a gun around at Crappers' Tavern shortly after their leaky old cruiser had run aground at Trappers' Cavern.

It was to that same tavern that Mr. Ross had repaired, after one last kite nap, for one last nightcap before heading home to his luminous spire. But a single nightcap is such a scrawny bore, and before long the "one" had become a brawny score. The Crappers' bartender—a spuminous liar but a frisky wench—poured out her hearts to him (she claimed to have been born with a pair) along with glass after glass of whisky (French). Inspired by the Abyssinian barmaid's ruminating lies (e.g., having once made porn with a bear) as well as the luminating ryes (which she mixed with salt water and called "sailor tea"), he took a perky quill and some sort of quirky pill then made like Samuel Taylor C—a man whose poetic notions, induced by noetic potions, were realized by scribbling while dreaming.

But barely had his scribbling and dreaming begun when it was interrupted by the untimely intrusion of a wandering Porlock wimp

---

(the two talents being, perhaps, in a psychoanalytic sense, analogous). What was discussed after Mr. Ross agreed to join them for a repast of the bivalve mollusks (to be swallowed alive according to the ever-beguiling vogue of gourmands) is not known, but the session involved enough prying and consumption to yield a stupefying clutter of empty shells.

When he returned overstuffed to the lighthouse—which had apparently been designed with only outside steps up to the observation and living spaces, making all entrances dramatic—he was in that state of bad-tempered happiness that somehow summons the impression of a blustery heron.

The odd thing about the lighthouse keeper was that he possessed a manner of speaking whereby he involuntarily jumbled words and phrases, sometimes to mildly comic effect. This verbal sabotage of meaning frequently spared those within hearing range of some exceptionally vile oaths and invectives, as well as some rather repulsive expressions of chauvinism and racism (never to be taken lightly, even when, as perhaps in this case, they do not reflect the true nature of their speaker but rather are an expression of social obliviousness bordering on the pathological). Except for the clearly unconscious nature of his transposed speech, such persistent inversion would surely strike the listener as an insistent perversion.

Not only was he oafish, but he may have been a bit of a birdbrain as well. For example, the first statement he made upon entering the interior of the lighthouse

whose sudden and startling appearance—he was dressed rather in the style of a warlock pimp—set the old lighthouse keeper to dribbling and screaming.

This boisterous oozing drew the attention of two daring shrinks who'd been sharing drinks and now invited him to join their oysterous boozing. (The duo had attained a degree of fame while shucking, though their true expertise was in treating individuals who experienced shame while fornicating.) By the time our Mr. Ross, eyes glazed as a dead hawk's, took his leave of the two head-docs, the battered shells of clamorous oysters lay all about him like the shattered bells of amorous cloisters.

Now back atop his familiar perch, with a belly full of oysterous regret, he burst through the lighthouse door like a roisterous egret.

"Great shucking fit!" he exclaimed. "It's raining bats and hogs out there!"

"It wasn't a bat," corrected the bosun, "just a natty bird blasted by a batty nerd."

Keeper Ross spun around with a look of awed shock, like a shod auk in Victorian sandals who'd been set upon by sick Taurean vandals.

---

was "It's raining bats and hogs out there." Now, if he was saying what he meant in this case, he was evidently—as the boatswain pointed out—misidentifying an albatross as a bat. Maybe it was just his boozy stupefaction, or maybe it *was* raining bats. We know it was raining hogs—well, one at least.

As for his sexism and crapulence—evidenced by the rude assumptions he made about his employee upon returning, which will not be repeated here—Ronna was quite willing to overlook both and indeed seemed even enamoured and amused by his conduct as she beseeched others, in a momentary spasm of linguistic contagion, to not "bind" her "moss."

Shauna was less inclined to overlook his behaviour, though given her almost existentially detached nature she wasn't about to wade too far into the issue, letting the matter go with a derogatory faecal reference cleverly parodying the lighthouse keeper's own flusterphonic style.

The boatswain remarked that, as lighthouse keepers go, this one was among the more disgusting and—the appraisal of a hobbyist psychotherapist, perhaps?—"repressively impulsive."

The captain, on the other hand, was sufficiently incensed by the lighthouse keeper's rudeness to Ronna that he proclaimed himself ready to fight were it not for the fact of his being a guest and therefore bound by certain rules of etiquette. (I will not venture to surmise which half of his personality was in place at the

"What the fiddling duck is going on here?" he squawked.

"He seems, ahem, like a pheasant plucker, doesn't he," said the navigator in a snide aside.

"I don't know about that," replied the first mate, "but if he mistook an albatross for a bat he's definitely not a bird watcher—more of a word botcher, by the sounds of it."

The keeper's gaze darted about the room like a hill grouse being chased by a chef at a grill house.

"And where's that busy ditch with the turkey pits I hired to feed all the crabby shitters? Out staking a troll like a trench fart with some boxy pumpkin or other strewn-muck casket base? Or maybe boffing queers like the Door of Heaven at some grub 'n' pill with a bunch of loot-beggars and other lolling bruisers? She's supposed to be here trashing my monk jail, lurking the womb, and mending the souls in my hawks! That boiled sprat is lamb ducky her moss is bellowing with age, otherwise—"

A florid hoot interrupted the snotty griping and grotty sniping as Ronna emerged through the crowd holding a shrill chimp she'd taught to chill shrimp. The sound was not from some horrid flute,

---

time of that observation.) Instead, the captain found himself happily distracted by the discovery of a tropical fruit that must have inhabited his breeches pocket for a considerable span of time, having by appearances long ago expired there and continued its residency as a fermenting corpse.

The first mate seemed shocked but not surprised when the captain lifted the ancient fruit to his mouth, and his advice—which clearly would not have been heeded anyway—came too late. "Oh, don't bite that fruit," he said, as if addressing, through a closed window or at too great a distance to be heard, a young child about to put a worm in his mouth.

The fruit was indeed so potently alcoholic that after only one bite, and despite his years of imbibing the most inebriating liquids concocted by man in the world's most depraved ports, the captain commenced to fling himself about the room in a hyperactive solo execution of a Latin American ballroom dance marked by melodramatic postures, extreme rhythmic shifts, and abrupt pauses.

The crew—who adored their skipper to a man but were often either frustrated by, or in hysterics over, his deportment—were shaking with laughter. And the small furry insectivore was a-tremble—but, again, one would have to be educated in the science and psychology of animal behaviour to discern whether that was from nervousness at the confusing outburst of energy in its surroundings or from a type of psychic or visceral resonance with the jocularity emanating from the crew, nor was it from Ronna's trusty sidekick who was then engaged in removing a crusty side-tick, nor from any of the other restive fauna, but from the suddenly festive Ronna herself. Rather than being disgusted by her employer—clearly a libelous boozer of a Bible-less loser—she seemed primly tickled by his supercilious blathering, superbilious slathering, and especially his frowzy diction (a trimly pickled form of drowsy fiction).

"Don't bind my moss," she began, before doubling over baftly as her laughter bubbled over daftly.

"Donna, my rear! What are you so jam dolly about? Why, the gore pearl is flickering so snakily she's tossed her lung!"

Indeed, as the lighthouse keeper observed, the poor girl was snickering so flakily she'd lost her tongue, but finally she managed to speak: "I mean, don't mind my boss—it's just that when he's in a drinking stupor he can be a real stinking drooper."

"He is a tit of a bird, isn't he," added Shauna. "And more than a bit of a—though I suppose everyone deserves the benefit of the doubt and I can hardly claim to be morally impeccable myself—turd."

"One of the more impressively repulsive, and repressively

---

with whom it had spent time at sea and thereby perhaps "entrained" to their emotional frequencies (amateur speculation, of course), or a third and admittedly more preposterous hypothesis: maybe the creature, in its mysterious way, simply thought the captain was funny as he danced convulsively about, bloodied and tattered, twisting and twirling in paroxysms of flamboyant passion, romantically dipping an invisible partner at breakneck speed, then shifting to petrifaction at the momentary discontinuance of imaginary music. Probably, though, it was just agitated by the noise in the room.

The lighthouse keeper, who was usually grim as someone who reaps the soft white fibres surrounding the seeds of a subtropical plant used to make textiles, also laughed. Then that sly dolt of a sentry stepped inside, droning like a medieval religious ascetic and moaning like a dipsomaniac who was no longer young but not yet old. He glanced psychotically at the crew, then, in the manner of a lackadaisical thief, scooped up the small furry insectivore and plunked it on the back of a chimpanzee who was holding a bowl of shellfish Ronna had taught it to refrigerate for consumption.

The degree to which this unexpected visitation surprised the monkey was evidenced by the sudden dropping of its jaw, so that it hung as slack as the mouth of someone experiencing the cessation of addictive craving upon the intravenous administration of a drug notorious for its stupendous opiate effect. But Ronna had

138

impulsive, lighthouse keepers we've met so far," marvelled the bosun.

"If I weren't a guest here, I'd fight that brute," snarled the captain.

"Oh, don't bite that fruit," implored the first mate. But it was too late: the captain had found in the pocket of his trousers—the ones with "Known on the Sea" sewn on the knee—an old tannic mango, so highly fermented that after only one bite he danced about the room in a manic tango.

The shrew began to quake as the crew began to shake with laughter. Even the rotten keeper, usually grim as a cotton reaper, joined in. Then the sluggish, onerous sentry made his luggish, sonorous entry, droning like a Middle Age monk and moaning like a middle-age drunk. Hoisting his gun he shot the crew a crazy look as he caught the shrew like a lazy crook and plopped it on the chimp's back.

The monkey's jaw dropped wide as a junkie's maw. Shamed by the true, if skimpish, urge to kill the impish scourge, he let his instincts be tamed by the shrew. Remembering the Golden Rule—having been force-fed by Ronna such olden gruel—he knew how not to do unto others: for those who are screamingly rude might in turn get reamingly screwed. And so as the Saviour Himself might

---

somehow taught the simian at least one of the tenets of Christianity—that you should treat others as you would have them treat you. So, in emulation of Jesus, the trained primate held up a shrimp—as if it were a pole made of copper-tin alloy—and offered it to the small furry insectivore. The odds were slim that the creature, accustomed to a diet of insects, had ever consumed shrimp before, but it took to the experience with relish, possibly because it had had little to eat for some time.

The crew seemed to take this as a cue to forget their manners and dived in as one, grabbing at the cold little sea monsters with all the refinement of hungry prisoners who'd been let out for the day.

Ronna admonished them, but the feeding frenzy continued noisily—seafood, we must conclude, being more appealing to these voyagers than cheese.

A knock at the door proved to be two police officers—one a swarthy fellow of German descent, exhausted from mounting the stairs, and the other an Orthodox follower of the Judaic faith who was appallingly congested from the effects of an influenza he'd caught from his partner. Ronna greeted them while frantically waving her hands behind her back, as if to simulate a two-handled air-blowing bag affixed for unknown reasons to a brothel's door. She expressed a wish that their evening was pleasurable, then inquired—obviously affected by the tumbled jock of her employer—as to what brought them to "our lusty old fighthouse."

have done, he lifted a shrimp from his bowl of prawns and held it aloft like a pole of bronze. Then the shrew on the chimp began to chew on the shrimp, and soon the whole crew joined in, grabbing at the cold prawns with all the manners of paroled cons.

"Mind the food rules, you rude fools!" preached Ronna. Then, hearing at the door a low knock, she turned and shouted, "Come in, there's no lock!"

Two officers of the law wriggled in like genial vermin, the one wheezing sneerily from the vertically spiral sloggy climb, the other sneezing wearily from the spurtically viral cloggy slime (he'd caught a blaring flu from his partner in flaring blue, an otherwise venial German).

"What's with the canned trout and the jealous zoo?" asked Keeper Ross, whose social graces were diminished by the smallness of both his cultural vortex and vultural cortex.

"Hello, officers," said Ronna, waving her hands behind her back like a bordello's door bellows in a futile effort to shush the crew. "I hope you're having an enjoyable evening. What brings you to our lusty old fighthouse—I mean, our fusty old lighthouse?"

---

Officer Faerber divined Ronna's intent with the posterior flapping gesture and assured her, as he removed his cap and exposed a toupee made of fur from a large mammal inclined to eating berries, honey, and occasionally humans, that he and his partner had not rushed ashore (for they were a special branch of the constabulary working closely with the Coast Guard) to make them keep the noise down. With regard to how their evening was going, he said it had been fine—prior to the brawl that broke out among women of a religious community living under vows of poverty, chastity, and devotion to the Lord.

Officer Goldbloom chimed in by mentioning the next incident that had required their attention: the sinking of a musical ensemble in a ridge of sand rising out of the water.

The chronological summary continued with Officer Faerber's reference to their having next discovered a merchant who had been murdered—and here the dark Rhine poet showed himself in Faerber—"with a knife to his slender vein." He was an elderly fellow who had a little store that sold, according to Goldbloom, everything from maize kernels meant to be exploded by heat and then snacked upon, to books and videos featuring police in such a way as to inspire sexual excitement.

The night, said Faerber, got even worse following that episode, when they had to wade through a dreary tract of wet muddy land to rescue from train wreckage a

"Oh, don't worry about the noise," said Officer Faerber, lifting his hat to reveal a rug made of bear fur. "We didn't rush ashore to make you shush a roar. And as for our evening…well, let's just say it was a fun night until the nun fight."

"And then that band sank in a sandbank," added Officer Goldbloom.

"That was just before we found that vendor slain with a knife to his slender vein."

"Yeah, an old guy with a shop called the Gold Eye. Sold everything from popcorn to cop porn."

"After that, things got even worse: next we had to wade through a dull bog on a rain trek to rescue a bulldog on a train wreck. He was a real bucking fighter, too, not to mention a f—"

"Gentlemen," interrupted Ronna, assuming the stance of a jock when a jock teases, "if you're not here about the noise, why *are* you here? Surely not to talk Jesus?"

"Actually, miss," said Officer Goldbloom, "we had a report that some stoned cocksucker shot a dolphin."

"I can honestly say," said Ronna honestly, "that no one here shot

---

squat, wrinkly-faced dog with powerful jaws. Despite their benign heroics, the dog put up quite a fight during the rescue operation—about which the officer had more to say, but Ronna infringed on his narration to imply, with a slight impatience in her voice and an almost taunting posture, that he should skip all that and get to the point of their visit. Though she might have liked otherwise, she presumed that they had not climbed the lighthouse steps to discuss the Son of God.

Goldbloom responded by announcing that they'd received a report about a drug-addled practitioner of fellatio having shot a dolphin. Quite possibly he was using a vaguely speculative, crudely vernacular expression to characterize the suspect, rather than being literal in his description (such specific facets of character being hard to glean by any witness, even under optimal conditions).

Ronna may or may not have known about the sentry's having shot a gentleman disguised as such a creature, but in either case she answered truthfully (so far as we know) that no one there—not even the gun-toting guardsman—had done such a thing. As she alluded to him, the sentry smiled like a fiendish corpse-eating pacifist master of a transcendental Eastern religion who had just consumed a ball-like portion of yellow-rinded Dutch cheese.

Tipping his uniform hat but leaving his skullcap in situ, Officer Goldbloom apologized for the bother and made to leave when he happened to recall a bit of literary trivia he thought the assembly might enjoy. It was regarding an allergic

a dolphin—not even Golding the Hun over there holding the gun."

The sentry smiled like a bashful nudist, or a gnashful Buddhist who, taking the form of a ghoulish Buddha, had just devoured a boulish Gouda.

"Well, sorry to bother you nice folks," said Officer Goldbloom, doffing one of his caps, then suddenly recalling a bit of trivia about a writer known for his bold gloom: "Say, did you know that snow peas made Poe sneeze?"

Before anyone could think to answer, the keeper of this high ribald haven—somewhat sobered but still swaying about like a wry highballed raven—piped up to say goodnight. "Now, I hate to drift off like a farting dog," he announced, "but tepee slime is upon me and I'm off to catch warty finks."

"The story of my life," said an awkward Officer Faerber, feeling erect from the reeling effect of being so high up—or perhaps it was the stinky whiff of fair Ronna and her rare fauna that made his winkie stiff.

"Just one other thing…" said Officer Goldbloom, like a niggling judge, as he gave his partner a jiggling nudge.

---

reaction said to afflict Edgar Allan Poe, causing him to violently expel air from his nostrils and mouth whenever he came in contact with a certain leguminous vegetable recognizable by its slender translucent pod.

There was a moment of tranquility as Ronna, Shauna, the sentry, lighthouse keeper Ross, and the crew, having finished the shrimp, contemplated this marvellous fact, a little unsure perhaps as to what response might do justice to such a fascinating intellectual tidbit.

The spell of awe and befuddlement was soon burst by the master of that spirited sanctuary-in-the-sky. Somewhat sobered by the appearance of the police but still swaying like a tipsy and sarcastic black bird of the very species immortalized by the aforementioned poet, Mr. Ross excused himself for bed, announcing, after his own style, that he hated to drift off like a darting fog but sleepy time was upon him and he was off to catch forty winks.

Officer Faerber, who had understood him to say that he was off to catch "warty finks," rejoined—with some temporary distraction arising from a condition of penile engorgement and stiffening resulting from either the vertiginous altitude or a hormonally charged olfactory reaction to the peculiar pungency of Ronna and the unusual creatures in her care—by saying that it was "the story of my life."

"One other thing…" said Officer Goldbloom, rather in the manner of an overly particular official who decides results in legal matters or competitions. As a

"Oh yes," said Officer Faerber. "Would you mind turning off that light? It's shining on the boats, and we wouldn't want a rash on our—that is, a crash on our rocks."

The sinful skipper was something of a skinful sipper. Having found his inlaid—or is that inlain?—satin flagon dry after flitting about like an insane Latin dragonfly, he had gone on a careless hunt in search of liquid treasure. Exploring the most remote nooks and crannies of the lighthouse, where only crooks and nannies had gone before, this prince of the ocean found not even a rinse of the potion he sought. The old Jack tar got his hopes up when he spied a bottle, but it was only an old tack jar. What he wouldn't give to find a jar full of booze, but—though he sought it with thimbles (in the manner of a snarking bellman) and thought it with symbols (in the manner of a barking Snellman)—there was not so much as a drop for this sage of ale from the Age of Sail. What he did find were the spoor and faeces of many foreign species, including a brute of a kitten that this coot of a Briton dressed in a mod ascot and pronounced his odd mascot.

And now, pushing his way through the crowd on the back of

---

mnemonic prompt, he lightly jabbed Officer Faerber's chubby ribs, snapping him out of his unfocused discomfiture.

"Oh yes," said Officer Faerber, recalling the matter they'd discussed as they approached the tower from sea. "Would you mind turning off that light?" He explained their concern that a nautical disaster might occur—"a crash on our rocks," to be specific—should the beam interfere with seafarers' ability to safely navigate the waters upon which it fell (just a safety precaution). As we will see later, the light remained on. Presumably, the job of illuminating the officers as to the purpose of a lighthouse fell to Ronna.

The wily captain had snuck off to look for hard liquor in the far recesses of the lighthouse. Though he sought it using the methodology proscribed by another great sea captain for the hunting of a certain species of fabulous creature, and after the more noetic approach that might have been favoured by an eminent Finnish philosopher of the nineteenth century (that is, sea captain's son Johan Vilhelm Snellman), he discovered not even a drop. Instead, he found the tracks and excrement of various exotic animals.

It was on the back of one of these—a leopard given to pushiness—that he rode back to his crew, drawing them together as would an affectionate overseer of woolly grass-eating mammals gather his excessively fond herd.

a shoving leopard, the captain collected his crew—like a loving shepherd gathering his doting flock—and led them down to the floating dock where their schooner lay moored.

On their way to the ship they encountered two vocal lawyers whom they mistook for local voyeurs. The men—prosecution attorneys moonlighting as exterminators—were debating flat fees for eliminating fat fleas and whether or not to charge treble hours for rebel towers such as the one that loomed before them: a lighthouse with encrested features, full of all manner of infested creatures. The sign on their van read: *Leacock & Keylock—Mitigating Lice and Litigating Mice Our Specialty.*

The captain, first to board ship, spotted a garish stowaway and fixed him with a stare-ish "Go away." This had no effect on the strange man in the dolphin suit, so the tiny Brit turned to his crew and demanded, "Who is this briny tit?"

"My name," said the stowaway, "is Sir Francis 'Frank' Raleigh, and I'm the victim of a rather rank folly. You see, I'd been invited to a mask ball at a Basque mall and I decided to ask our maid what I should wear to this masquerade. She suggested I attend as a courtly

---

He then led them down the spiralling stairs of the lighthouse to the buoyant pier where his ship (which for no apparent reason was called the *Spooner*) lay anchored and tethered.

Along their route they passed a couple of noisy legal practitioners who at first appeared to be peeping Toms. On some metaphoric whim, no doubt, these courtroom predators were operating a side business as paid destroyers of insects and rodents. Their confidence and expertise in this secondary field may have been less than infallible, as the promotional slogan on their vehicle stated that one of their specialties was in merely "mitigating" a certain form of parasitic insect and that the other—relying heavily on their professional background—was in serving legal notices to small furry pests whose numbers tend to prevail despite much more forcible means of eviction, such as poisoning and trapping. They seemed to be preparing for the job of ridding the lighthouse of the multiple infestations associated with its resident wildlife.

Upon boarding the ship, the captain noticed a gaudy trespasser who would have been decadently attired even without the dolphin costume. It was, of course, the first of the two unlucky fellows presumed to have been ruthlessly murdered by the sentry. He had, in fact, suffered only a surface wound by virtue of all but one of the marksman's bullets—and that one striking obliquely—missing their target. It was not the first misfortune of this odd gentleman's evening: the

porpoise, so we thus attired my portly corpus. Having granted a night off to my bodyguard—a Sherpa from Persia who'd gone to hear some gaudy bard—I set off from our yacht alone. When my dinghy snagged and began to decompose on a rock, all I could do was swim for shore in the hope I might recompose on a dock. That's when my plan of frolicking among sinful gentry was shot down by a ginful sentry—a coltish vassal in that voltish castle over there. Yes, some sassy ass of an asinine assassin ass-assassinated me. Though the bullet that marred me merely grazed my butt, it may as well have braised my gut, for I sank like a jogging lamb in a logging jam. Fortunately, I managed to grab hold of a stretcherous length of cable attached to your weighty anchors, which I clutched with the lecherous strength of eighty wankers. I then pulled myself to safety above the greedy waves and weedy graves of drowned seamen.

"There was, by the way, another victim who was not so lucky: some loony sobster who was wailing and waving a sail that I think read something like *SAVE THE SUNNI LOBSTER!*"

"So I take it you want a lift back to the yacht," said the

---

reason he'd been swimming for shore is that the dinghy in which he'd embarked from his yacht had ripped on a rock and deflated. Normally, he would have been accompanied by his bodyguard—a Nepalese mountain guide who had lived for some time in Iran—but the fellow had been granted a free evening to attend a poetry reading by some author with a tastelessy showy, overblown, and exasperatingly decadent style. His purpose in leaving his ship—and this explains the dolphin outfit, as well—had been to attend a fancy masquerade party at an indoor shopping complex exclusively featuring shops marketing products and services from a serene yet politically tumultuous region of northern Spain that extends along the Pyrenees into France. Alas, his hopes of indulging in some naughty fun with the class of people nearest the aristocracy were dashed when a glancing shot scraped his posterior. Despite the superficiality of the injury, he sank like a meek quadruped trotting on a congestion of logs bobbing in a lake whose arboreal shores were being harvested by the lumber industry. It was only thanks to a burst of energy, seemingly sparked by a kind of autoerotic fury in the face of imminent death, that he—Frank was his name—managed to hoist himself to safety via the anchor rope of the schooner. He also mentioned, in case the captain or his crew might care, that he was not the only one who'd been inconvenienced by sniping: a blubbering ninny who'd seen him splashing about like a dying cetacean after the dinghy's demise had come to his rescue (with a

navigator, a man accustomed, from many undignified sea tours, to unsignified detours.

"I'm not fussy, really," replied Frank, absently adjusting his dorsal fin by tugging at his hole. "Wherever you happen to be going is fine—as long as the locals don't shoot me and there's tea with crumpets; and of course when I soak my crumpets in tea it's always nice to hear trumpets in key, so as long as there's a quay with trumpets—Gnostical trumpets—and maybe some Saxon flutes played by nautical strumpets in flaxen suits, I'll be quite content. As long as there are Fijian wigs and Ouija and figs, and—oh!—some of those Turkish mints with the murkish tints; as long as I can sip Vanilla Mirandas on Manila verandahs with Geishan hosts and Haitian ghosts; as long as there are Iberian lynx I can sketch with Liberian inks, and Brahmans in shambles and shamans in brambles chewing bollocksome frondage that transports them into a sort of frolicsome bondage (like those jungle fellows who eat fungal jellos then go into dotty trances while disporting themselves in trotty dances); as long as there are pine forts where I can drink fine ports after Incan meals of mink 'n' eels; as long as there are..."

---

banner Frank mistakenly recalled as having read *SAVE THE SUNNI LOBSTER!*) and had been fatally shot for his troubles.

The navigator seemed less interested in the particulars of the stowaway's tale than in whatever additional bother his presence might entail. "So I take it you want a lift back to the yacht," he said, his perfunctory tone betraying a hint of weary resignation.

Frank replied that he was happy to tag along wherever they might be going. "I'm not fussy," he said, before elaborately inventorying the extraordinary and exotic sensory delights he would modestly anticipate along the way. Just as he specified something about a hog feast, the same pig that had fallen from the lighthouse scampered up the ramp and joined them on deck.

Seeing the pig, the pushy leopard made a charge straight for it. The captain clung for dear life as the ungainly cat took off in clumsy pursuit, chasing the boar across the beautifully filigreed grain of the floorboards. The squeal of the pig as it tottered on the brink of exhaustion (really, it had had quite a day) rose above the voices of the first mate and the navigator, who were clutching the wheel and arguing—the captain himself being otherwise engaged—about what course to set.

It was into this mad chaos that Shauna, after descending the steps of the lighthouse, cast her lot. This newest member of the crew proposed a voyage that,

When he got to the part about sherry-showered boars roasting on berry-bowered shores, up trotted the pig itself.

The bumbling feline, with the captain still astraddle, made a fumbling beeline for the pearly swine and chased it across the swirly pine of the deck. The pig let out a squeal and began to wobble while the first mate and the navigator grabbed the wheel and began to squabble about where to sail next.

And as the leopard gave the boar a shove, and the lighthouse shone on the shore above, a tourist stepped aboard the ship, with a splendid plan for a nautical trip.

"I hear Siberia is nice this time of year," said Shauna, "if you go by Syria."

*The End*

---

while quite impossible, was no more outlandish than many previous seafaring escapades aboard the *Spooner*.

And so they set sail again, this strange society—but of their fate beyond this point we know nothing. We can only hope that Shauna quickly found her sea legs and is free of nausea, that the pig and the leopard are getting along without serious mischief, that the navigator has chanced now and again upon a lawful cure for celibacy, that the captain's antics have not endangered the lives of his crew or himself, and that the winds of delirious fortune will blow ever favourably the sails of their little ship.

*The End*

# Glossary

*absquatulate* to beat an opponent so badly he leaves growing in clusters

*albatross* a sacred book dealing with the adventures of rogues

*art* a short punch delivered by supernatural means

*asthmatic* a tubular organ used to fasten glass in sashes

*axiom* an outrageous, shocking, offensively indecent picture or design too small to be seen by a microscope

*Aztec* a card game in which the first player to get rid of his cards hangs from the ceiling to address with abusive language a group of aquatic invertebrate animals

*berserk* any of several large, erect-eared, bushy-tailed doglike predatory mammals that are destructive to any of numerous small eight-legged blood-sucking animals from this or that place

*Bohemian* a person or thing that can roll itself into a clot of slimy substance in order to avoid duties or dangers

*burka* a small horse used in the examination of internal organs for purely selfish ends

*catalepsy* a neurotic state marked by sticky and hairy long distance radio transmissions

*charlatan* a person or persons pulled up and down a slope by high tension electric power lines to stimulate the sexual organs when all desire is extinct

*convalescence* the belief that there is no God within the Arctic and Antarctic circles

*cranium* a zoological garden or collection of animals being under the influence of alcohol or a drug

*craw* the cavity between the lips and throat containing a trap for catching mice

*crumpet* a sound suggesting a small black-and-white bug destructive to handwriting

*dolour* sickness that results from a wistful yearning to commit sodomy with a mythical monster slung under a dirigible balloon

*dunderhead* a generally elongated depression of land caused by a short prayer at a meal

*dervish* one temporarily fulfilling the functions of a large North
    American deer related to the tuna

*dramaturgy* the belief that spirits of the dead communicate with
    two kinds of anteaters that are very bad

*Dymaxion* a jet engine that operates on the same principle as
    a continuously fluttering or vibratory device connected to
    an arrangement of ropes and pulleys that hangs below the
    waist of a ferocious flesh-eating animal propelled through the
    air by a whirling windstorm created by a jet engine that
    operates on the same principle

*enthrallment* an emptying of the bowels, having to do with the
    mental state in which consciousness seems to expand

*euphoria* an abnormal, often irresistible, impulse to stop what one
    is doing

*glyptodon* a kind of shrub eaten on holy days

*grenache* language that appears to be meaningful but in fact is
    a syrup-like solution made by boiling several hormones fatal
    to spiritual progress

*hedonist* a person who suffers torture or death for the sake of a
    coil-shaped fossil shell

*intaglio* an abnormal dread of any burst of a number of things
    at once

*jigsaw* a dance in which couples two-step, balance, and twirl
    vigorously, tending to explode

*kama sutra* the fleshy part attached to the rear edge of an
    airplane's wing

*Komodo* a woman who uses her charms and tricks to enter into and
    reanimate a dead body

*kraken* a small round cake made of something startling and unreal

*lechery* an extreme impulse to act like an unskilled labourer who
    trifles with drone pipes

*lexiconjury* any doctrine or religious movement that advocates
    shameful wickedness with the alphabet

*lighthouse* a reverberatory furnace in which the soul becomes a
    fabulous animal

*lucid dreaming* to pass the summer in a state of torpor induced
    artificially by motor-driven resonators and metal tubes
*maelstrom* a severe outbreak of senseless veneration
*manatee* a person filled with excessive and often misguided
    enthusiasm for a small conical pile of hay
*manta ray* a military weapon that throws a stream of sweet opaque
    jelly made from bones, hoofs, and skin
*marzipan* the portion of the brain and spinal cord which,
    when placed between the teeth and struck by the finger,
    foretells the future
*nausea* having sexual feeling for a small earthenware jar
*ovarian* a person who plays the small organ at the anterior or
    ventral part of a megalithic tomb
*pneumatic* a decorative lacelike pattern suggesting luxuriant and
    succulent moral depravity
*quaver* a wavy lustrous pattern capable of being seen when viewed
    from the seat of the soul
*rapture* the highest stage of religious enlightenment, characterized
    by dizziness and often death
*sasquatch* a noxious, pestilent plant inducing luxurious languor
    when eaten in a silk tube covered with wet organic material
*schmaltz* a kind of popular American music given off by stars
*schnauzer* an otherwise respectable public official who hunts
    a small farmer or farm labourer for the purpose of scientific
    investigation
*schoonerist* a person trained to take care of people who are
    excessively or foolishly fond of tinkling metal discs
*sleep* the act, process, or method of not producing music
*sofa* meaningless, complicated, or obscure ritual having no worth,
    value, dignity, or importance in which one aims a revolver at
    one's head and plays the harp with a tomahawk
*spelunker* a surgical appliance worn by a composer of sacred poems
    to frighten children into obedience
*spermatozoon* an intimate nightclub for excessively luxuriant
    insectlike animals employed to secure adequate supplies of the
    clear colourless transparent jelly used by druggists to desecrate
    the church

150

*spiral agitator* a snake that kills its prey by emitting a viscous translucent substance in a sudden copious stream

*spoonerism* a song of joy or praise having to do with a freshwater fish that lives on human flesh

*sprocket* a man-made oblong fruit that explodes when thrown against a hard surface

*squall* a pilotless ship or airplane controlled by inordinate indulgence in sexual activity

*Stropharia cubensis* language or action intended to mystify or confuse a member of the middle class of society

*stupefaction* psychiatric treatment by means of a signalling system that uses different positions of arms, bars, or flags

*synaesthesia* a game for amusing a baby in which one repeatedly hides a vacuum tube under the armpit of a large leaping marsupial mammal supported by two long poles, the forward ends of which are fastened to a battery attached to a smooth-coated dog balanced on the upper back portion of a carcass whose ends alternately rise and fall

*tango* spiritual illumination by delirious fury

*thespian* an inhabitant of a colony engaged in fighting a ten-armed mollusc that breeds in Arctic regions with greedy or malicious pleasure

*Transvolcanic Plateau* a district of the city into which the intestinal, urinary, and reproductive canals all empty

*vacillation* the art of stuffing a marine cephalopod with dark, glossy, iridescent tropical fruit or entrails

*winkie* a small whirlpool made by a cat when it is contented

*zequox* a dangerously fascinating formation of clouds causing sleepiness in children

# Uncommon Sense Revolution:
# The Whirled View of Steve Venright

*Alessandro Porco*

> I believe in domains of existence vivid and compelling beyond
> even this miraculous reality we call the world.[1]
> —Steve Venright

> ...the first duty of a political activist is to become psychedelic.
> Otherwise you're not making your moves cognizant of the
> entire field of action.[2]
> —Terence McKenna

No city in North America had a more active rave scene than
Toronto in the early 1990s. Suburban teens travelled into the city
for the music and the drugs, joyously dancing—in small clubs, large
warehouses, or carnivalesque open-air venues—from Saturday night
to Sunday morning.

Production companies such as Exodus, Chemistry, Nitrous,
and Pleasure Force organized and promoted events. The style and
size of events varied from Exodus's all-age parties at 23 Hop to
Chemistry's extravagant *20,000 Leagues Under the Sea* theme night.
In 1992, X-Static opened at 162 John Street, selling imported DJ
mixtapes, paraphernalia, clothing, and event tickets. CFNY, CIUT,
CKLN, and Energy 108 broadcast music and popularized DJs such
as Don Berns, DJ Iain, Dr. No, Malik X, and Chris Sheppard. Zines
began to appear—*The Communic8r*, *The Punter*, *Transcendance*.
Even a Toronto Police Service task force put an ear to the bass-
thumping ground.[3]

In the Toronto Police Service files, you may find a passing
reference to Canadian poet Steve Venright, creator of the Alter
Sublime Hallucinatorium. Inspired by William Burroughs and
Brion Gysin's Dreamachine, the Hallucinatorium was a "touring
neurotech sideshow engineered to provoke retinal splendour in the
unwary."[4] (The sideshow was named after Christopher Dewdney's
long poem "Alter Sublime.") Venright set up the Hallucinatorium

at Toronto raves in the early 1990s, offering patrons special "sessions"—or *trips*—with names like Turbulation, Tranceport X, and Velvet Airlines. As Venright explains,

> Visitors to the nomadic Hallucinatorium were treated to designed and improvised stroboscopic stimulation by means of the D.A.V.I.D. Paradise, a superb light-and-sound device developed and manufactured by Comptronic Devices Ltd. The therapeutic applications of this instrument are quite remarkable, but so are its properties as a catalyst of spectacular visual phenomena. By programming sequences that exploited the Paradise's most dynamic and varied effects, I was able to produce a sort of intracranial fireworks display for those who donned the patented Omniscreen eyesets. For many, the experience went beyond the enthralled observation of fascinating colours and patterns to become a hyperlucid and ultravivid dream of otherworldly aspect.[5]

Semi-clothed ravers sprawled on loveseats, lawn chairs, and chaise lounges, devouring the Hallucinatorium's "illegally beautiful images," which both the law of realism and the real law could never detain, question, or arrest.[6] Venright became known, affectionately, as "the trip-out man" with his "mindfuck machines."[7]

The Hallucinatorium, however, is only one of the many ways Venright has explored "the edge of sanctioned reality."[8] Since the late 1970s, he has relied primarily upon the techne of language—as advanced as the D.A.V.I.D. Paradise and organic as any entheogen—to represent the phenomenology of psychedelic experience, publishing five volumes of poetry as well as numerous chapbooks and broadsides. *The Least You Can Do Is Be Magnificent: Selected & New Writings* demonstrates Venright's sustained and focused commitment to "the utterly Other," with a heady mix of dream visions, psychonautical adventures, and verbal hijinks.[9] At every turn, he populates his real and imaginary landscapes with what André Breton calls *le merveilleux*, conjuring aliens, chimera, fairies, and ghosts, as well as unknowable and unnamable hallucinations.[10] This career retrospective collects the very best of

Venright's work in the continued fight against reason, logic, and common sense.

Steve Venright (né Wright) was born in Sarnia, Ontario, on September 16, 1961. Sarnia is a border city located in the southwestern-most point of the province, approximately 96 kilometres north of Detroit, Michigan, and 293 kilometres west of Toronto. The Blue Water Bridge crosses the St. Clair River, connecting Sarnia with Port Huron, Michigan. The iconic bridge is the local source of Venright's early Orphic interest in crossing borders—between poetry and prose, animal and human, beauty and terror, literature and music, analog and digital formats, and sound and sense.

Sarnia's suburban neighbourhoods are surrounded by the natural beauty of Lake Huron, Canatara Beach, and the Bright's Grove Sewage Lagoons. However, the smokestacks of petrochemical plants and refineries also distinguish the city's skyline. In the years after World War II, the Canadian government invested in Sarnia's petrochemical industry, creating "the Chemical Valley," at the centre of which is Polymer, a federally owned plant that manufactures synthetic rubber. (In 2011, the World Health Organization declared Sarnia's air the most polluted in Canada.) Sarnia attuned Venright to the ways in which the natural and synthetic are always interfused.

Venright enjoyed the usual comforts of growing up in a loving home. Nevertheless, he suffered the acute miseries of adolescence, especially as a teen interested in the surreal, psychedelic, and alien. An untitled poem from Venright's high school years reads, dramatically,

> I'm a razorblade wristwatch
> I'm a handgun cigar
> I'm a noose-rope necktie
> At the suicide bazaar

The young Venright composed under the influence of Blake's vatic voice, Breton's oneiric imagery, Alice Cooper's schlock horror, and Pink Floyd's art rock. He wrote poems with titles like "The

Magnificent Nightmare," "The Liquids of Sleep," and "When Butterflies See Mirrors," as well as an unpublished "vérité novel/memoir" from 1978-79 with the Sartre-inspired title *The Other Side of Despair*.[11] He stapled and shared photocopies of his work with friends and teachers. For a while, he even adopted "Stewart Venright" as his nom de plume, an anagrammatic reordering of "Steven Wright" with the witty addition of "art."

Venright was first published in 1981 in *ABC's of Creative Writing*. The anthology included his poem "The Hôtel La Salle." One year later, in February 1982, at twenty, he moved to Toronto, where he's lived ever since. Venright's move to the big city resulted in inspiring and collaborative literary friendships with iconic figures such as jwcurry, Nicky Drumbolis, Daniel Jones, and Stuart Ross. He discovered a community of like-minded artists devoted to making and sharing poetry. His poems soon began to circulate around the city in a special issue of the *Poetry Toronto* newsletter edited by bpNichol and through jwcurry's Curvd H&z broadside series. Venright recalls, "Those were great days for a young poet, hanging out at This Ain't the Rosedale Library and Letters Bookshop, where there was always a lot going on, and getting in on the scene at 9 Davies Ave., where the Four Horsemen and Owen Sound would perform in the Kontakte series."[12]

A bibliographic history of Venright's poetry grounds his poetics in Toronto's small press scene of the 1980s and 1990s. Poet-critic Clint Burnham defines the "small press" as a social "network" of collaborators distinct from, and opposed to, "the mainstream of capitalist publishing."[13] It exists on a more intimate scale of production that's "almost rigorously unprofessional" and yet, at the same time, artisanal.[14] Friends and lovers share the burden of labour with the author. Single individuals often assume responsibility for multiple tasks, such as design, editing, and printing. Materials are "borrowed" from day-job supply rooms on the hush-hush: mimeograph machine, computer, printer, paper stock, photocopy machine, paper trimmer, sewing fabric, stapler, stamps, and envelopes.[15]

Small press publishers create broadsides, zines, chapbooks, and full-length books that, in design, oppose standardized formats and large-scale manufacturing.[16] Every occasion of publication inspires a reconsideration of the relationship between form and content. Burnham believes "such publishing posits a radical critique of the ways in which our world is bought, packaged, and sold, and makes a utopian gesture to a world where individuals will control their own labour, instead of selling it, [along] with their dreams, to others."[17] Of course, these publishing practices result in literary ephemera that's difficult to find and expensive to buy. Thus, *LYCDBM* ensures that Venright's extraordinary writings are not limited to the shelves of antiquarians and archivists. It also reveals that, like a true Surrealist, Venright has from the start been committed to protecting his dreams and owning his labour.

The earliest poems in *LYCDBM* ("The Grace," "My Examination," and "Possessions") were written between 1983 and 1985, and they first appeared in *Visitations*, Venright's debut collection. Like many of his French idols (Lautréamont, Baudelaire, Michaux), Venright is fiercely loyal to the prose poem. The paragraph—as opposed to the line—is the prosodic unit of measure in the book's tales of suburban terror. He focuses on obscure, unnamable forces that disturb the superficial tranquility of manicured lawns and domestic bliss in southwestern Ontario.

Underwhich Editions published *Visitations* in 1986. Like Coach House Press, Underwhich adopted an "editorial collective" model: individual editors assumed responsibility for finding manuscripts and ushering them into book form. The founding members of the collective were Michael Dean, Brian Dedora, Paul Dutton, Steve McCaffery, bpNichol, John Riddell, Steven Ross Smith, and Richard Truhlar. Dean selected *Visitations* for publication after hearing Venright perform with Nicholas Power and jwcurry at the Groaning Board Restaurant.

Stuart Ross typeset the book on an AM Varityper CompEdit 5900 in the offices of York University's student newspaper, while Venright was responsible for the book's graphics and design, including the cover image. It foregrounds a chimera—part bear, part raccoon, part rabid dog—superimposed over a dissection manual and a map of the Kenora region, a sparsely populated area of northwestern Ontario known for its harsh climate, ancient lakes, and dense wilderness. The figure of the chimera is Venright's symbol of the unknown.

Animals populate his early tales. In "Possessions," for example, the taxidermied remains of an unclassified chimera are the source of paranormal activity that compels a fearful young couple on "the border of hysteria" to flee their home. Here, Venright plays with the tropes of horror fiction and cinema. In "Carcass," a sympathetic couple try to rescue an injured animal on the sidewalk, only to be warned off by a grumpy police officer who simply wishes to have it removed to the dump heap by a garbage man. The officer's brutish behaviour demonstrates a lack of care for the suffering animal—that is, a lack of imagination.

The unknown is also associated with the dark of night and, thus, dreams. The book's title poem, "Visitations," presents a young man whose dreams are filled with an unending procession of shape-shifting animals; like Magi, they bring him "haunting gifts." In the harrowing "My Examination," the narrator describes a dream of imprisonment and torture. He's subjected to a series of "test[s]" by his captors, who are referred to as "instructors." The prisoner is expected to recite a "soliloquy" as fellow inmates heckle and a stampede of amphetamine-injected pigs races toward him. He refuses, and the dream ends as he's surrounded and threatened by a "deep, vicious growling at [his] feet." The dream suggests some childhood trauma connected to the discipline-and-punishment model of educational institutions and the experience of glossophobia. The prison imagery calls to mind such human rights violations of the twentieth century as Chinese and Russian re-education camps.

Venright's first major poem, "The Grace," weaves together themes of obsession and possession—to hunt *and* to be haunted. A young couple wake one morning to discover their living room has been ransacked. They don't know why it has happened or who is involved. A "little hunt" ensues. Like a pair of amateur sleuths, the couple attempt to piece together the scattered clues. They are assisted by a group of unnamed friends and acquaintances, equally perplexed by what's happened. The poem depends upon a single metaphoric conceit: memory is imagined as a "dissevered cobra." As the narrator explains, "No matter how diligently we sought… we couldn't seem to find the head or the tip of its other extremity, the tail. We still had no idea of the creature's full size, of how much there was still to recover." The poem is ostensibly a whodunit and, fittingly, it has a noir-ish feel.

On the one hand, the couple is desperate to put the "serpentine jigsaw puzzle" together.[18] They want to determine what happened, to fix memory and meaning in place. On the other hand, it's impossible to restore that which is lost or destroyed, as the couple is well aware: "the whole matter of such a reconstruction suddenly seemed comical." Such perspective on the matter is, however, fleeting. The desire to know, name, and define returns just as suddenly—and tragically. So, once more, the couple sets off in search of answers. The prose form of "The Grace" is rhythmically structured around this constant movement between "distress and euphoria."

In 1990, Toronto-based couple Clint Burnham and Katy Chan started Contra Mundo Press, publishing limited-edition broadsides and chapbooks by Gil Adamson, Kevin Connolly, and Stuart Ross. Burnham and Chan published Venright's *Notes Concerning the Departure of My Nervous System* in 1991. It was intended as a promotional item to drum up interest in Venright's second full-length book, *Torpor Vigil*, which Contra Mundo had also agreed to publish. But when Burnham and Chan separated, the press shut down, leaving *Torpor Vigil* in limbo.

A small collection of eleven prose poems, *NCDNS* is best considered a transitional book. Venright experiments with a variety of rhetorical genres (instruction manual, warning label, tour guide) and formal structures (the list, chiasmus, anaphora), many of which he later employs with far greater facility and purpose, especially in *Spiral Agitator*.

The chapbook's design epitomizes Burnham's theory and practice of the small press. It's formatted like a compact disc booklet and fits perfectly into a lidded jewel case. There's an album cover insert and a back card, which lists numbered tracks (i.e., poems). The cover image is a detail from one of Venright's paintings, *Variegraph #127*. This musical design suggests new protocols of performance and reception for poetry. As the instructional note on the back card states, the poems are "TO BE READ AT MAXIMUM VOLUME."[19] *NCDNS* is loud, urban, and angry.

The poem "Cosmic Lace" introduces a central figure in Venright's "whirled view": the cyclone or tornado. The cyclone is Venright's symbol of the imagination as a dialectical force. Like Yeats's gyre, it's beautiful and terrifying, creative and destructive, still and in motion. The spiral figure appears in many later Venright poems, including "Timetwister," "Thunderheads," "The Deregulation of Nature," "The Spiral Age," "Region X-4S-10C," "Cybervac 2000," "Spiragitalation," "Rotatiga Larips," "Stations," "Somnibus (A Rotary Oratory)," and "Manifesto of Indiscriminate New Glory." It's also dominant in Venright's visual art, especially his variegraph series: *Neuralchemy*, *Spiral Agitator*, *Topomorph*, and *Chaosat*. The variegraphs look like drunken mandalas—dizzying twists, turns, slurs, and tumbles of fluorescent colours.

"Ode to Joy" and "Scenes from Childhood" continue to explore dreams and early childhood trauma, respectively. In the former, Venright filters the Greater Romantic Lyric through Pink Floyd. It begins, "Many years ago, in the middle of the night, I was very sick. As I slept, I dreamt that my stomach pains were being caused by an autoharp embedded in my abdomen." In Venright's mock ode, the modern autoharp replaces Coleridge's Aeolian harp, and Keats's "beauty is truth, truth beauty" chiasm takes a darker, gastronomic turn: "pain can sometimes make us dream of beauty, but that beauty always awakens us to our pain." "Scenes from Childhood" (like "My Examination" and, later, "Jar") provides an especially unsentimental look at childhood.

But the best poem from *NCDNS* is "What You Need to Know." Venright assumes the persona—and sweater-vest uniform—of a docent, guiding patrons through the exotic home of Madame Tapir, who sounds straight out of a novel by Zola or Maupassant. Her curious home is equal parts hotel, art gallery, and theatre. Visitors are both actors and spectators as they walk the corridors. With each sentence, the docent matter-of-factly reveals the unusual goings-on associated with Madame Tapir's, where nothing is quite as it seems: "Voyeurs are encouraged to use the infra-red binoculars provided at no extra charge by the management, although these are not permitted on the third balcony which overlooks the fabled 'Courtyard of Deception.'" Venright's docent in "What You Need to Know" is a prototype for his later xenagogic narrators.

*Straunge Wunder; or, The Metalirious Pleasures of Neuralchemy* was published a full decade after Venright's debut.[20] Here, Venright's writing moves away from tales of suburban terror and toward altered states of consciousness—meditative trances, reincarnation, drug-induced trips, mesmerism, sexual ecstasy, and, in particular, "the fantastical realm of lucid dreaming." Venright displays increasing mastery over multiple rhetorical genres, parodying the infomercial, instruction manual, and travel guide. He also begins to locate and access the Other in the play of signs. Puns, portmanteaus, compound words, idiosyncratic spellings, and advertising jingles add a light touch to the dark and heavy hand of his early symbolism.

*SWMPN* is the first of only two perfect-bound books published by Natalee Caple and Brian Panhuyzen's Tortoiseshell & Black Press. Caple recalls that she received a modest $1,000 arts grant to start the press and publish Venright's book in an edition of five hundred to six hundred copies. The short-lived press (1996-98) focused on publishing "hand bound chapbooks and broadsides" to sell at book fairs or trade as part of poetry's gift economy. The enterprise dissolved when Caple and Panhuyzen divorced.[21]

*SWMPN* is a gorgeous book thanks to Caple and Panhuyzen's design (e.g., the use of forest-green endpapers), Stuart Ross's editorial guidance, Eric Gill's Perpetua typeface, Coach House Printing's Zephyr Antique Laid paper, and especially Richard Kirk's illustrations. Venright and Kirk met as teenagers in Sarnia and became fast friends. *SWMPN* is Kirk's first major publication, though he'd later collaborate with horror-fiction luminaries Clive Barker and Thomas Ligotti as well as Nu metal band Korn. Kirk's work is primarily "monochromatic," using "ink, silverpoint, and graphite," and it shares stylistic affinities with the illustrations of Mervyn Peake, Maurice Sendak, and William Heath Robinson.[22] *SWMPN*'s cover shows a suited businessman who has washed up on the rocks of an unknown land where he encounters a woman holding a lemur that's feeding at her breast, a one-eyed donkey that walks upright, and a fish-brained—literally—dwarf chef. Kirk's drawing dramatizes what happens when Herbert Marcuse's one-dimensional man bears witness to multiple dimensions.

*SWMPN* includes "Border Dissolution '94," one of Venright's most iconic poems.[23] In "Nonnational Boundaries of Surrealism," André Breton explains that "the liberation of the human spirit" and reclamation of the imagination's rights must involve "writers and artists of all countries," including Canada, where Breton travelled in August 1944.[24] Surrealism transcends the modern nation-state's sentimental boundaries, educational institutions, and language academies. It's not beholden to the regime of waking life. Instead, it advances a heterodox program of creative action—on the street, on the page, on the canvas—based on dream imagery, chance operations, and automatism: "It is only when the fantastic draws near, at a point where human reason loses its control, that the innermost of a human being has every chance to express itself."[25] Surrealism is not an aesthetic but a way of being. Any citizen alive to the marvellous's consciousness-expanding power is a threat to national security.

A road-trip poem, "Border Dissolution '94" is Venright's first explicitly political work. Two Canadian writers from "Turrawno" are en route to Sherman, New York, to attend a conference on "consciousness."[26] They're vocally hamming up a quaint CBC Canadian-ness for the customs officer with a "crocodilian head." Their "sombre reptilian interrogator" asks about the writers' visit, but the answer is neither "business" nor "pleasure": "We're just comin' over to shoot a few people then going right back." The answer is Venright's homage to the "Second Manifesto of Surrealism," in which Breton infamously proposes, "The simplest Surrealist act consists of dashing down into the street, pistol in hand, and firing blindly, as fast as you can pull the trigger, into the crowd."[27] (A copy of the manifesto is, in fact, in the car's back seat.) The U.S. customs officer reacts to the answer as if it's perfectly reasonable. The poem's painful irony is an indictment of the U.S. Constitution's Second Amendment and the American cultural obsession with guns. It's simple: guns maintain borders, and consciousness dissolves them.[28]

*SWMPN* is also significant because, for the first time, Venright's poems invoke Torpor Vigil Industries, the 'pataphysical business venture he started in 1991. Originally, TVI produced "fine art prints and clothing."[29] However, it soon developed into "an organizer of literary salons, a purveyor of neurotechnology, [and] an instigator of outlandish social maneuvers."[30] The Alter Sublime Hallucinatorium was, for example, one division of TVI: applied research in psychedelics. TVI was also responsible for the Mobile Reality Inspection Lab: in October 2000, as part of the 7a*11d International Festival of Performance Art's StrangeWays program, the lab "hit the streets of Toronto to conduct a series of 'reality checks' aimed at determining the density and quality of reality at various institutions, residences, businesses, government offices, and public spaces."[31] Crew members walked the city in lab coats, Tyvek suits, and protective eyewear like mad scientists, ghost hunters, and performance art provocateurs. Such parapoetic projects teeter on the brink of scandal and absurdity, yet Venright is absolutely serious and gleeful about them.

In "Lucid Dreaming Reality Test," Venright markets TVI's Mobile Reality Inspection Lab's program:

1. Telephone any branch of the Federal Government. If your call is answered, you are probably dreaming. If it is answered by someone other than an alleged government employer—a museum curator, perhaps, or a hair salon receptionist—check the number and dial again.

Think of Venright's "exercises" as a sort of inspired CrossFit for the imagination. In "An Introduction to Your New TVI Septal Electrode™," Venright's vocal flare mimics that of an infomercial pitchman. He promotes a new "model" electrode that "allows friends or loved ones to transmit euphoriagrams from any location within a three-kilometre radius." In "Thunderheads," he fabricates mass-market thunderstorms with names as quirky as MAC lipstick colours: consider "Imperial Skycruncher."

Venright's most popular and thematically cohesive book, *Spiral Agitator*, was published in 2000 by Coach House Books. It represents the mature synthesis of surrealism, psychedelia, and agitprop. Venright's Spiral Agitator is an H. G. Wells–like invention. It takes ontology for a ride on the *Gravitron*. It spins being into Being, terror into the sublime, and torpor into grace. The Spiral Agitator translates the Hallucinatorium's "auralchemy" from the rave to the page and from the dance floor to the Word Processor. It is a living, organic machine that dreams, revealing a "secret phenomenological truth": "that the World is determined by imaginative volition." Venright is no longer content to merely investigate or theorize the possibility of altered states and other worlds. He wants to invent, map, and experience them. The poet becomes a cartographer of the imagination.

There's no better example of this development in Venright's poetics than "The Black Domain," a work in the tradition of Swift's *Gulliver's Travels*, Verne's *The Mysterious Island*, Carroll's *Alice in Wonderland*, and Jarry's *Exploits and Opinions of Dr. Faustroll, Pataphysician: A Neo-Scientific Novel*. The title alone brings to mind Breton's "The Black Forest," Dante's "selva oscura," and Rauschenberg's Black paintings.

The poem's conceit is simple, but it provides Venright an occasion to showcase his ingenuity. An unnamed scientist delivers a lecture—accompanied by a slide show of twenty-six photographs—to an audience of skeptical academics. Slide by slide, he describes the eponymous "Black Domain" or "Forest of Blackness" in detail. The museum docent of "What You Need to Know" is now the xenagogue of "The Black Domain," though the Virgilian guide isn't in a Tuscan forest but an antiseptic hotel conference room.

Reading "The Black Domain" is a lot like watching an episode of *Ripley's Believe It or Not!* There's a definite rhythmic movement between the oohs and ahs of childlike wonder and the cynical guffaws of professionalized adults. The Forest of Blackness is monochromatic, with shades and gradations of black from charcoal to jet. Like deep space, it is absent of sound. Fruits look and feel like fruits on earth, but they are flavourless. The snakes have no eyes, and the dogs are so still they're confused for statues. The Forest of Blackness is governed by its own laws of physics. And it's entirely synthetic.

In one of the poem's most dazzling passages, the scientist describes entering a hidden grotto, wherein he discovers a large wall—as ancient and magical as the Chauvet Cave in Southern France or the Cave of Altamira in Spain—with multicoloured 3-D hieroglyphs that, through the power of telepathy, are in fact the projected words and images living in, and moving through, his mind exactly as he thinks them, though (paradoxically) they are not his thoughts. At this moment of encounter, he has a "quasi-religious" or "mystical" experience and faces a crisis of epistemic faith in the cave. "The Black Domain," then, is as much about satirizing the rhetoric of authority in scientific discourse as it is about celebrating the power of imagination and mystery of alterity.

*Spiral Agitator* is Venright's most political book. It was composed during the first term of Mike Harris's contentious premiership in Ontario and the rise of the Conservative Party's "Common Sense Revolution," which included senseless cuts to social assistance, health care, education, and the arts. Poems like "The Long and the Short of It," "The Unedited Word of God," and "The Deregulation of Nature" are among Venright's best works in this mode.

In "The Long and the Short of It," Venright sums up the worst parts of the twentieth century, including colonialism, capitalism, ecological disaster, religious fundamentalism, technodeterminism, and political corruption. The poem is comprised of eleven discrete tercets, making it one of Venright's rare lineated poems. Each stanza presents a variation on the classic *good news/bad news* joke: "The good news is…" (setup), "The bad news is…" (punchline), and "The result is…" (tag):

The good news is that the government has fallen.
The bad news is that it has fallen on *us*.
The result is that everything will always be the same forever
    (not that it ever wasn't).

In "The Unedited Word of God," Venright uses a popular biblical aphorism ("it is easier for a camel to pass through the eye of a needle than for a rich man to enter the Kingdom of Heaven") to critique the unequal distribution of wealth. He is attracted to the aphorism because it's an example of proto-Surrealism: the camel and needle occupy "two distant realities," with incommensurate scales of being.[32] The difference, when juxtaposed, produces what Breton calls *"the light of the image."*[33] Venright generates increasingly bizarre scenarios by introducing paradigmatic substitutions into the biblical aphorism's syntactic structure:

a ruby-throated hummingbird to unscrew the lid of a ketchup
    bottle…
a wombat to jump the Grand Canyon on a tricycle…
a praying mantis to milk a cow…
a rhinoceros to do a jigsaw puzzle of the Taj Mahal…
a fruit fly to laugh…

With "The Deregulation of Nature," Venright turns his attention to the politics of nature. Evoking Alan Liu's provocative statement "There is no nature," TVI happily markets a series of modifications to nature:[34] moving organisms into new, unexpected environments; instigating controlled weather phenomena, such as tornados; and even creating and meeting the "pharmacological needs of various insects, arachnids, and cephalopods." At the same time, Venright recognizes that such a utopian project depends entirely upon the logic and language of neoliberalism—poetry, nature, and the imagination are never free from economic interests.

Formally, *Spiral Agitator* showcases Venright's increased reliance on the inventory or list form, as in poems like "Nuevocations," "Malpractice," "The Unedited Word of God," and "What Happened." Venright's use of the list is something he shares with Stuart Ross, whose inventory poems include "Burial," "The Uneven Century," "Bulletin," and "The Catch."[35] For Ross, the list is ethical: a way of giving an account of oneself. For Venright, the list is formal: a problem of repetition and variation. His goal is to solve the problem with ease and wit.

The design of *Spiral Agitator* cleverly plays with anxiety surrounding the transition from paper to digital formats of publication in the late 1990s, while also challenging generic codes of the book, transforming the back cover from an advertising space to a pedagogical one. The meaning of this design is inextricable from the history of Coach House Press and Coach House Books.[36]

Plenty has been written already about the inspired origins of Coach House Press and, ultimately, its demise in the mid-1990s.[37] In short, the press's cooperative model of publishing got pushed out by a corporate model. According to Frank Davey, everything at the press simply got "too big": "Growth, after all, is the primary ideological assumption of capitalist economies. Without growth there are no new jobs, no dividends for stockholders, no income from the stock market holdings of one's RRSP."[38] The capitalist economy—underwritten by the meddling in the arts of federal and provincial government agencies—overwhelmed the gift economy. This had an effect on the aesthetics of the book, and Coach House Press became "just another extruder of standard books."[39] Darren Wershler recalls that management discouraged "experiments with physical form," such as "embossing, foldouts, inserts, colour, [and] new media."[40]

In 1996, Coach House Press closed its doors due to the burden of debt, cuts to arts funding, the rise of big-box stores, mass returns of overproduced titles, misguided sales and marketing campaigns, and the cost of paying professional, salaried employees. But by March 1997, original founder Stan Bevington and poet Victor Coleman had already reopened the press under the name Coach House Books. They had a new, improved, and appropriately scaled mandate: to produce "small initial runs of finely printed books, coupled with more or less simultaneous electronic editions."[41] They talked with writers about how form and content might converge or diverge in the book's print and digital editions. Throughout the late 1990s, Wershler and web developer par excellence damian lopes created an online archive of over seventy digital books, including *Spiral Agitator*.

The paper edition is unusually small and boxy at 13.97 cm x 16.19 cm. Like *NCDNS*, *Spiral Agitator*'s cover features Venright's own artwork: *Variegraph #88*. The endpapers include black-and-white details of another variegraph. In lieu of marketing bumf, friendly blurbs, or pull quotes, the back cover is a list of over one hundred invitees to an imagined poetry gathering. The audience includes all "Children of the Turbulation, Fleurs du Mal, Lucid Dreamers, Hunters of the Snark, Surrealists, Recordists…Mushroom Goddesses, Surfers of the Timewave, Entheogenerators, Soluble Fish, Sleeptalkers, Green Men…Shamans, Boundary Dissolvers, Aboriginal Voices…Underworld Magicians, Orphic Revellers, [and] Maldororians," among many others. Venright uses the back cover to announce his earthbound and cosmological influences. His list of invitees is pedagogical, teaching us how to read and receive his work.

Venright also incorporates the very fact of his linguistic text's double existence into the paper and digital editions, demonstrating what media theorists Jay David Bolter and Richard Grusin refer to as "remediation."[42] He includes a hilarious "Troubleshooting" guide at the back of the paperback, providing solutions to various "glitches" in the book:

> *Problem:* No picture. No sound. VCR making growling noise.
>
> *Probable cause:* Book has not yet been made into a movie.
>
> *Solution:* Wait several months then inquire at your local video rental shop. If *Spiral Agitator* is still not available in video format, reinsert book and make the most of it. Adjust tracking.

Similarly, in his "A Note on the Text," Venright provides an exhaustive gloss on the material history of the book's making: "These words, with few exceptions, were initially written using a series of Pilot Hi-Tecpoint V5 Extra Fine markers with an anti-gravity feature that enables the author to write while supine... The text from 1998 was processed in Microsoft Word 60 on a PowerMac desktop coupled with a Vu-Sonic 17ps low-radiation monitor..." Both the "Troubleshooting" guide and "Note" draw attention to and celebrate the process of translation from medium to medium—another example of Venright's interest in the poetics of the border.

Since 2000, Venright has published one collection of poetry, 2007's *Floors of Enduring Beauty*, with Toronto's Mansfield Press. (The title is a punning play on Baudelaire's *Fleurs du Mal*.) In terms of design, the book is the most ordinary and streamlined of Venright's career. The remediation conceit of *Spiral Agitator*, illustrations of *SWMPN*, and punk iconoclasm of *NCDNS* are conspicuously absent. Nevertheless, *FEB* remains significant as a small press artifact because it represents the culmination of Venright's lifelong creative friendship with Stuart Ross.

In 2007, Denis De Klerck, founder and owner of Mansfield, hired Ross to acquire and edit poetry manuscripts for his press. One of Ross's first editorial decisions was to publish *FEB*.[43] Venright's nonsense verse, surreal narratives, and self-help satires presented a radical and welcome departure from Mansfield's back catalogue of the early 2000s, which included books of poetry by Pier Giorgio di Cicco, Matt Santateresa, Corrado Paina, and Christopher Doda, for example.

More than his previous collections, *FEB* is a showcase for Venright's remarkable sense of humour. The book is light, optimistic, and funny. It's filled with adventure, both in terms of the stories Venright tells and how he tells them. The horror and fantasy tropes of *Visitations* and *SWMPN*, respectively, have diminished significantly. Venright explains,

> At certain other times in my life, there's been more gravity behind the impulse to write. As I get older, I seem to be more geared toward just having a blast with it. My instinct for humour took over during the writing of *FEB*… Humour is one of our most transformational tools. If used just right it can be equally good for toppling oppressive regimes and breaking the ice at parties. Just because something is humorous, it should be noted, doesn't mean it isn't "serious."[44]

Sure, Venright has mellowed with age; however, he remains committed to "toppling oppressive regimes."[45] What's different is his methodology. Puns, spoonerisms, found text, and scatology locate Venright's poetry "in the presence of laughter."[46] As Baudelaire writes in his prose poem "The Desire to Paint," it is "the laughter of a wide mouth, red and white and alluring, that makes one dream of the miracle of a superb flower blooming on a volcanic soil."[47] Like dreams, laughter instigates an encounter with the Other. In addition, Venright's prose poems in *FEB* are now much longer: for example, his ten-chapter novella "The Tin of Fancy Excrements: A Journey of the Self" and his spoonerist masterpiece "Manta Ray Jack and the Crew of the *Spooner*."

Poems like "Beautiful Thoughts," "Distended Aphorisms," and "One Hundred and Seventeen Steps to Instant Gratification" satirize to great effect the bestselling genre of self-help literature—from Dale Carnegie's modern classic *How to Win Friends and Influence People* and Werner Erhard's New Age philosophy in *The Mind's Dedication to Survival* to Chelsea Clinton's *It's Your World: Get Informed,*

*Get Inquired & Get Going!* and your local Chinese takeout joint's fortune cookies. The rise of the lyric poem and the rise of self-help literature are historically contiguous phenomena. Venright makes this correspondence explicit, conferring the predatory practices of the huckster upon the poet and, by extension, suggesting that lyric poetry is nothing more than an emotional Ponzi scheme that preys on the vulnerable. In this sense, the contemporary poet is closer to Scientology founder L. Ron Hubbard than to Arthur Rimbaud.

The aphorism is a genre of writing that communicates universal truths (in short, memorable sentences) that may, in turn, be applied to particular occasions. Aphorisms magnetize our collective moral compass. But the aphorism, says Auden, is "essentially an aristocratic genre of writing. The aphorist does not argue or explain, he asserts; and implicit in his assertion is a convention that he is wiser or more intelligent than his readers."[48] In "Distended Aphorisms," Venright simultaneously assumes and mocks the aphorist's ungrounded authority. His sentences are a little too bloated to be pithy, and they argue for an uncommon sense, emphasizing practical survival rather than spiritual transcendence: "Pissing in one's shoes will not keep one's feet warm for long, but it's a surefire way to get out of a bad date."

"The Tin of Fancy Excrements: A Journey of the Self" continues the self-help satire. It follows the misadventures of a bumbling unnamed hero on an "aimless" quest to discover a "mystery [he doesn't] even care about." He traverses a post-apocalyptic Ontario, encountering government-funded performance artists, the camp of a "paramilitary neo-hippie security squad," and a strange town wherein all the signs are marked by metathesis. "The Tin of Fancy Excrements" is the love child of Robert Desnos's *Liberty or Love!* and Cormac McCarthy's *The Road*. The novella suggests that self-discovery is nothing more than a MacGuffin—with a monthly payment.

But the crowning achievement of Venright's career is "Manta Ray Jack and the Crew of the *Spooner*," a high-seas, low-humour adventure in the nonsense modes of Lewis Carroll and Dr. Seuss. A newly revised and expanded version of the poem is presented in *LYCDBM*.

The plot is simple: Captain Manta Ray Jack and his crew anchor their ship, the *Spooner*, on an island—not unlike the Island of Cack in Jarry's *Dr. Faustroll*—and, subsequently, visit the local lighthouse's pub in search of food and drink. What follows is an evening of tall tales, sexcapades, and scatological fun. The primary source of joy and laughter when reading the poem is that every sentence includes *at least* one spoonerism:

> Far below, where sea grazed coast, the creeping beam wandered like a crazed ghost, lighting in the livid purview of its vivid purlieu a series of seaside scenes, to wit: a mock duck and a dairy fox covered in dock muck on the ferry docks; a brash hick hawking his wares (a hash brick) while walking his hares; a fawn buyer and a lane mobster at a bonfire eating Maine Lobster™ (*"hand-caught and canned hot!"*); a cab driver and a crab diver discussing the tipping of rides and the ripping of tides; a skinny troll with a musty funk stealing a tinny scroll from a fusty monk; two glamourous imps exchanging an amorous glimpse after pining in the dark while dining in the park; and a pretty girl with a Yorkie puppy admiring a gritty pearl with a porky yuppie. Also visible in the roving light was a sprawl of schoonerists whose ship, now docked, was covered in the scrawl of spoonerists.

The associative winds of the spoonerism set the story in motion, so that language, in fact, is the central character in the story. Each sentence's rhythm is physically felt in the anticipation and realization of the phonemic inversions.

However, that's only one aspect of the poem's elaborate structure. Venright divides each page horizontally in two. On the top half, he provides the spoonerist rendering of Captain Manta Ray Jack's exploits. On the bottom half, he offers an overly literal, hyper-rational translation of those same events:

> Far below, where ocean met shore, the sweeping luminosity meandered like an insane spectre, lighting on its way the following seaside scenes: a mallard decoy and a lactophilic canid enslimed on a pier from which a small carrier boat makes its regular voyage to a nearby island and back; a bold

rustic lad selling a resinous psychoactive block while exercising his bunnies; a purchaser of young female deer and an alley gangster at a controlled outdoor blaze eating delectable canned crustacean meat from the east coast of the USA; a taxi operator and an underwater hunter of certain other tasty carapacious life forms gabbing to each other about gratuity protocol and hazardous currents; a slender and dankly odorous cave-dwelling gnome absconding with a metallic roll of parchment belonging to a stuffy old-fashioned member of an insular male spiritual commune; a couple of alluringly chic mischievous sprites expressing libidinal inclinations, each toward the other, at the conclusion of a repast within the perimeter of a public green space; and an attractive young woman holding a baby Yorkshire terrier while observing, in the company of a chubby urban professional, the beauty of a sandy but lustrous accretion manufactured by an otherwise unindustrious aquatic bivalve. Another thing revealed by the traversing beam was the haphazardly dispersed crew of a schooner at anchor, which appeared to be decorated in the graffiti of dyslexics.

In terms of genre, the bifurcated page scores a crosstalk comedy routine. The bottom half serves as the deadpan "straight man" to the top half's nonsensical "funny man." "Manta Ray Jack and the Crew of the *Spooner*" is a text that performs on the page like a classic vaudeville duo: Flanagan and Allen, Abbott and Costello, and Smith and Dale. In terms of politics, the bifurcated page evokes the linguistic relation of colony to Empire: the carnivalesque nonsense of the former (Outlaws) and the Standard English of the latter (the Law).

Now in his mid-fifties, Venright continues to write poetry and, with less frequency, publish it. Part Two of *LYCDBM* includes a small selection of new and previously uncollected materials. Poems like "Incidents of Exposure" and "Other News" are similar to Venright's earlier inventory poems, with an added emphasis on reportage. His poems respond to the increased homogenization of news media as well as the glibness with which the various horrors of the twenty-first century are reported. "Beyond Me" and "Some Common and Not-So-Common Similarities" harken back to the witty formalism of *Spiral Agitator*. Venright also continues to explore light verse with "Plight of the Urban Sasquatch and Other Limericks." (The earliest limerick in *LYCDBM*, "The Man from Southampton," was composed circa 1990-92, the result of an afternoon of creative play with his young son, Kerry.) Finally, in "David McFadden Trip," Venright describes a fantastical road trip—in a "Dymaxion Model T" automobile—with beloved Canadian poet David W. McFadden.[49]

In "The Grace" (discussed earlier), a young married couple try to figure out how and why their home's been mysteriously looted. There's mention of a "landscape painting" that hangs, decoratively, on the living-room wall. The painting is likely of the local-colour variety, purchased at the farmer's market early one Saturday morning along with a jar of organic honey, heirloom tomatoes, and apple pie hot out of the oven. It's as pleasant, competent, and innocuous as the furniture in the room, though definitely less Swedish. Or maybe the artwork is a bit more sophisticated: a print by Tom Thomson, Emily Carr, or one of the Group of Seven—the Romantic ideology of landscape in mechanically reproduced brush strokes across the national canvas.

But this "landscape painting" has been vandalized. First, the ordinarily level and anchored frame now hangs at a "disconcerting angle." The angle defamiliarizes the painting and, by extension, the nation. The spatial reorientation inspires confusion, surprise, and uncertainty. How do we make sense of this new, different landscape? Second, the painting is "curiously slashed." A knife or, more likely, some chimera's adamantium claws have torn a hole in the canvas and, by extension, in the history of representation and the representation of history. For the couple, this is an especially violent act with little regard for the so-called morals of the nation and the anodyne decor of the middle-class living room.

Looking into this askew canvas reveals, perhaps, the nation's legacy of colonial violence against Indigenous peoples. This is the "dark side of the landscape," to quote John Barrell.[50] The "curious slash" cuts into the metanarrative of Canada, and the painful history of the Other spills out: the Aamjiwnaang First Nations people who live in the middle of Sarnia's Chemical Valley. Or the tear opens to *another* room, a large gallery space with examples of the kind of non-representational Canadian art that's almost *never* showcased on our stamps or in our schools—for example, the Painters Eleven of Oshawa, Ontario. Or the "curious slash" is the gateway to imaginary landscapes: Thomas Cole's heavenly city, H. P. Lovecraft's Dreamlands, Edgar Rice Burroughs's Barsoom, Jules Verne's mysterious island, Walt Disney's Tomorrowland, L. Frank Baum's Oz, Guillermo del Toro's labyrinth, and Venright's own topomorphic fields and moth grottos.

The tear in the fabric leads away from the "consensual reality domain" and toward the unknown and impossible. Sometimes it's terrifying; sometimes it's beautiful. On occasion it's even hilarious. Whatever the case may be, for almost forty years, Steve Venright has been our trusty guide: Virgil with glow sticks, a whistle, and DMT.

*The Least You Can Do Is Be Magnificent* is a real trip.

### Notes

1. Steve Venright, "Statement," in *Surreal Estate: 13 Canadian Poets Under the Influence*, ed. Stuart Ross (Toronto: Mercury Press, 2004), 168.

2. Terence McKenna, *The Archaic Revival: Speculations on Psychedelic Mushrooms, the Amazon, Virtual Reality, UFOs, Evolution, Shamanism, the Rebirth of the Goddess, and the End of History* (New York: HarperCollins, 1992), 13.

3. See Denise Benson, "Rave Archives," *Then & Now—Toronto Nightlife History*, accessed May 1, 2016, thenandnowtoronto.com; *The Communic8r: A Chronological Trip through the Golden Age of Raving in Toronto*, accessed May 1, 2016, www.thecommunic8r.com; Kyle Grayson, "The (Geo)Politics of Dancing: Illicit Drugs and Canadian Rave Culture," in *Chasing Dragons: Security, Identity, and Illicit Drugs in Canada* (Toronto: University of Toronto Press, 2008), 197-236; Trent Lee, "Ten Signs You Were a Toronto Raver in the 1990s," *BlogTO*, last modified August 24, 2015, www.blogto.com; Mireille Silcott, "Toronto, Canada: Hardcore Anglophilia and Jungle's Northern Exposure," in *Rave America: New School Dancescapes* (Toronto: ECW Press, 1999), 75-98.

4. Steve Venright, "Alter Sublime Neurotechnologies," *Torpor Vigil Industries*, accessed May 3, 2016, torporvigil.com.

5. Ibid.

6. Ibid.

7. Steve Venright, "Last question for today," email to author, May 21, 2016.

8. McKenna, 3.

9. Ibid., 12. For the sake of brevity, Venright's longer book titles will be abbreviated. The first time a book is mentioned, the full title will be used; all subsequent references will be abbreviated:

> *LYCDBM (The Least You Can Do Is Be Magnificent)*
>
> *FEB (Floors of Enduring Beauty)*
>
> *SWMPN (Straunge Wunder; or, The Metalirious Pleasures of Neuralchemy)*
>
> *NCDNS (Notes Concerning the Departure of My Nervous System)*

10. André Breton, "Manifesto of Surrealism," in *Manifestoes of Surrealism*, trans. Richard Seaver and Helen R. Lane (Ann Arbor: University of Michigan Press, 1969), 14.

11. Here are the opening sentences of *The Other Side of Despair* (MS):

> The words return empty to me. Have not been sustained by the consciousness into which I woke. It was an unconsciousness, I mean. I fall back now, fall back far using these things of communication. Description gone. Metaphors random, useless. There is no communication. Cellophane—everything. Can't explain. Will write anyway. Will write all day maybe. Stay in one spot, only movement of pen, and natural oscillation of guts. Action would only lead me to play along—I'd only be defeating myself. No precision in these layers of reality and even less when automatically/arbitrarily transcribed by your drifting faculties. (Steve Venright, "Other Side of Despair," email to the author, July 9, 2016)

12. Steve Venright, "Second installment of notes," email to the author, July 13, 2016.

13. Clint Burnham, *Allegories of Publishing: The Toronto Small Press Scene* (Toronto: Streetcar Editions, 1991), 6.

14. Ibid., 9

15. See Beverley Daurio, *Internal Document: A Response to Clint Burnham's Allegories of Publishing: The Toronto Small Press Scene* (Toronto: Streetcar Editions, 1992); Stuart Ross, "In the Small-Press Village: New Trends in

Adequate Stapling," in *The State of the Arts: Living with Culture in Toronto*, ed. Alana Wilcox, Christina Palassio, and Jonny Dovercourt (Toronto: Coach House Books, 2006), 254-62.

16. Burnham, 12-13.

17. Ibid., 19.

18. Venright's interest in puzzles with missing pieces dates back to *The Other Side of Despair*, in which he writes,

> But like a puzzle, my mind says, maybe if I talk and talk the pieces which initially seem vastly scattered will in time be more complete—the spaces will close up a little, but not absolutely of course. Standing back, the illusion you observe in reading this might—but so unlikely is this—scatter your own little puzzles. But my 'puzzle' has no edge, no defining contour.

19. "TO BE READ AT MAXIMUM VOLUME" is Venright's variation on the back cover of David Bowie's *Ziggy Stardust* album, which includes the instruction "TO BE PLAYED AT MAXIMUM VOLUME."

20. *SWMPN* includes many of the poems Venright had initially planned to include in the abandoned *Torpor Vigil* collection.

21. Natalee Caple, "Question about STRAUNGE WUNDER," email to author, May 20, 2016.

22. Richard A. Kirk, *The Art of Richard A. Kirk*, accessed April 28, 2016, www.richardakirk.com.

23. For the purposes of this essay, I will use Venright's updated title, "Border Dissolution '94," which locates the poem in the year of its composition. However, when the poem first appeared in *SWMPN*, it was simply titled "Border Dissolution."

24. André Breton, "Nonnational Boundaries of Surrealism," in *Free Rein*, trans. Michel Parmentier and Jacqueline d'Amboise (Lincoln, Nebraska: University of Nebraska Press, 1996), 9.

25. Ibid., 13.

26. The poem is based on Venright's trip to the 1994 Starwood Festival to see Terence McKenna.

27. André Breton, "Second Manifesto of Surrealism," in *Manifestoes of Surrealism*, 125.

28. The poem was included in the anthology *The Common Sky: Canadian Writers Against the War*, ed. Mark Higgins, Stephen Pender, and Darren Wershler (Toronto: Three Squares Press, 2003). Post 9/11, "Border

Dissolution '94" acquired new meaning as a form of protest poetry in the Age of Bush and Cheney.

29. Venright, "Alter Sublime Neurotechnologies."

30. Ibid.

31. Steve Venright, "Reality Check," *Rampike* 12, no. 1 (n.d.): 18.

32. Breton, "Manifesto of Surrealism," 20.

33. Ibid.

34. Alan Liu, *Wordsworth: The Sense of History* (Stanford: Stanford University Press, 1989), 104.

35. See Stuart Ross, *Hey, Crumbling Balcony! Poems New & Selected* (Toronto: ECW Press, 2003).

36. *Spiral Agitator* is Venright's only book with Coach House Books. However, it's worth noting that both *Visitations* and *SWMPN* are printed by Coach House. *SWMPN*, in particular, has the look and feel of a Coach House publication from late 1990s and early 2000s.

37. See Stephen Cain, "Imprinting Identities: An Examination of the Emergence and Developing Identities of Coach House Press and House of Anansi Press (1967-1982)" (PhD Diss, York University, 2002); Victor Coleman, "The Coach House Press: The First Decade. An Emotional Memoir," in *Coach House Press, 1965-1996*, spec. issue of *Open Letter: A Canadian Journal of Writing and Theory* 9, no. 8 (1997): 26-35; Frank Davey, "The Beginnings of an End of Coach House Press," in *Coach House Press, 1965-1996*: 40-77; Darren Wershler, "NICHOLODEON: epitaph," in *Coach House Press, 1965-1996*: 99-114.

38. Davey, 72.

39. Coleman, 34.

40. Wershler, 105. See issues of Wershler's zine *Torque* (1995-98) for the kinds of "experiments with physical form" he describes, e.g., oversized folios and red paper.

41. Ibid., 107.

42. Jay David Bolter and Richard Grusin, *Remediation: Understanding New Media* (Boston: MIT Press, 2000), 45.

43. A few years earlier, in 2004, Ross also published Venright's poetry in *Surreal Estate: 13 Canadian Poets Under the Influence* (Toronto: Mercury Press, 2004).

44. Steve Venright, "The Great Canadian Writer's Craft Interview: Steve Venright," interview by Nick, *Open Book: Toronto*, last modified June 3, 2013, www.openbooktoronto.com.

45. Ibid.

46. Jean-Luc Nancy, "Laughter, Presence," in *The Birth to Presence*, trans. Brian Holmes et al. (Stanford: Stanford University Press, 1993), 368.

47. Baudelaire, "The Desire to Paint," quoted in Jean-Luc Nancy, *The Birth to Presence*, 370.

48. W. H. Auden and Louis Kronenberger, foreword to *The Faber Book of Aphorisms* (London: Faber & Faber, 1962), vii-viii.

49. The remarkable poem serves as an excellent complement to Stuart Ross's poem about David W. McFadden, "Some Kind of Slowdown in the Intersection." See Ross, *Hey, Crumbling Balcony!*, 141.

50. See John Barrell, *The Dark Side of the Landscape: The Rural Poor in English Painting, 1730-1840* (Cambridge: Cambridge University Press, 1983).

# Notes to the Poems

ABBREVIATIONS

*FEB*—*Floors of Enduring Beauty* (Toronto: Mansfield Press, 2007)
*NCDNS*—*Notes Concerning the Departure of My Nervous System*
    (Toronto: Contra Mundo Press, 1991)
*SA*—*Spiral Agitator* (Toronto: Coach House Books, 2000)
*SWMPN*—*Straunge Wunder; or, the Metalirious Pleasures of
    Neuralchemy* (Toronto: Tortoiseshell & Black, 1996)
*VIS*—*Visitations* (Toronto: Underwhich Editions, 1986)

"Lighting the Towers (Author's Foretext)": The "Invocation
of Resonant Forces" list first appeared on the back cover of *SA*.
Reprinted as *A Neureality* (Toronto: Martin Garth Press, 2000).
Revised and expanded between November 2000 and May 2017. The
remainder of the introduction was completed in August 2016.

PART ONE: SPIRAL AGITATORS AND OTHER STRAUNGE
WUNDERS (1983-1999)

"Transvocations": First published in *Public* 20 (2000), p. 21.
Included in *SA*, pp. 106-7. Originally titled "Nuevocations."
    "My Examination": Included in *VIS*, n.pag.
    "Counting Cars": First published in the "Phenomenology" issue
of *Rampike* 6.2 (1988), p. 68. Included in *NCDNS*, n.pag.
    "Ode to Joy": Included in *NCDNS*, n.pag.
    "The Grace": First published in the anthology *Visitations*
(Toronto: Gesture Press, 1984), which included individual works
by jwcurry, Nicholas Power, and Venright, as well as jwcurry's
collaborations with Mark Laba, Steven Smith, and George Swede.
Other Venright poems in the anthology include "Gifts" and "The
Detection." *Visitations* was produced on the occasion of a multimedia
performance by the authors at the Groaning Board in Toronto (131
Jarvis Street), where Venright worked as a waiter. Included in *VIS*,
n.pag. Revised July 2016.
    "Possessions": First published in *Other Channels: An Anthology*

*of New Canadian Poetry*, ed. Shaunt Basmajian and Daniel Jones (Toronto: Associate Members of the League of Canadian Poets, 1984), p. 10. Originally titled "Fetish." Included in *VIS*, n.pag.

"What You Need to Know": First published in *WHAT! Contemporary Writing and Ideas* 25 (Nov./Dec. 1990), pp. 13, 15. Included in *NCDNS*, n.pag.

"Scenes from Childhood": Included in *NCDNS*, n.pag.

"Jar": Included in *SWMPN*, p. 23.

"The Long and the Short of It": First published in 1998 as a "little stapled chapbook" by Nicky Drumbolis's Underdog / Letters Press. In 1999, Coach House Books published a broadside edition on the occasion of the Mercer Union's "Faking History" show, which included Venright's variegraphs; other artists included Daniel Bowden, Hanna Claus, Angela Inglis, Grant McConnell, Sally McKay, and Alison Norlen. The Coach House edition of "The Long and the Short of It" is subtitled "A Millennial Report from Torpor Vigil Industries." Included in *SA*, pp. 17-19.

"Border Dissolution '94": Included in *SWMPN*, pp. 15-16. Reprinted in *Burning Ambitions: The Anthology of Short-Shorts*, ed. Deborah James (Toronto: Rush Hour Revisions, 1998), p. 14. Reprinted in *The Common Sky: Canadian Writers Against the War*, ed. Mark Higgins, Stephen Pender, and Darren Wershler (Toronto: Three Squares Press, 2003), p. 93. Originally titled "Border Dissolution."

"An Introduction to Your New TVI Septal Electrode™": Included in *SWMPN*, p. 33.

"Lucid Dreaming Reality Test": Included in *SWMPN*, pp. 21-22.

"Changeless": Included in *SWMPN*, p. 45.

"What Happened": First published in *Public* 19 (2000), pp. 94-95. Originally titled "Ledger." Included in *SA*, pp. 30-31. Reprinted in *side/lines: A New Canadian Poetics*, ed. rob mclennan (Toronto: Insomniac Press, 2002), pp. 257-58.

"The Unedited Word of God": Included in *SA*, pp. 52-53. Reprinted in the chapbook anthology *Can't See the Poems for the Trees* (Toronto: BookThug et al., 2002), pp. 18-19; the chapbook was printed on the occasion of a poetry reading on December 8, 2002, in London, Ontario.

"The Last Invitation of Summer": First published in *The Edges of Time: A Celebration of Canadian Poetry* (Toronto: Seraphim Editions, 1999), pp. 182-83. Included in *SA*, pp. 60-61. Reprinted in *FEB*, "Six Epistles," pp. 40-41. Translated into French and reprinted as a broadside by B. Bennett Thompson and Louise Doyon for a reading on December 18, 2008.

"Malpractice": Included in *SA*, p. 59. Reprinted in *New Canadian Poetry*, ed. Evan Jones (Markham: Fitzhenry and Whiteside, 2000), p. 84. Reprinted in the chapbook anthology *Can't See the Poems for the Trees* (Toronto: BookThug et al., 2002), p. 17; the chapbook was printed on the occasion of a poetry reading on December 8, 2002, in London, Ontario. Reprinted in *The Boneshaker Anthology*, ed. Lillian Necakov (Toronto: Teksteditions, 2015), p. 137.

"The Deregulation of Nature": Included in *SA*, pp. 55-58. Reprinted in *The Boneshaker Anthology*, ed. Lillian Necakov (Toronto: Teksteditions, 2015), pp. 138-39.

"Sentence": Included in *SA*, pp. 26-27. Reprinted in *New Canadian Poetry*, ed. Evan Jones (Markham: Fitzhenry and Whiteside, 2000), p. 83. Originally titled "Smargana Lareves."

"The Serpentine Dance": Included in *SA*, pp. 114-15. Originally titled "Epilogue: The Serpentine Dance."

"The Black Domain": Included in *SA*, pp. 83-104. Reprinted in the "Science Fiction" issue of *dANDelion* 31.1 (2005), pp. 8-16.

PART TWO: FLOORS OF ENDURING BEAUTY AND OTHER FINE QUALITY REALITIES (2000-2016)

"Transvocations Two": Additional entries to the "Nuevocations" series, which first appeared in *SA*, pp. 106-07.

"The Tin of Fancy Excrements: A Journey of the Self": Included in *FEB*, pp. 59-71.

"Beautiful Thoughts": Excerpts first published in "Somnibus (A Rotary Oratory)" in *SA*, pp. 70-71, and "Is" in *SA*, p. 35. "Is" ["È"] later appeared in the anthology *Toronto Venezia*, trans. Barbara Del Mercato (Venice: Studio Chestè, 2003), p. 3. An excerpt was also included in an untitled piece from the anthology *Very Short Stories*, ed. Josh Thorpe (Toronto: Off the Cuff Press, 2003), p. 48. Included in *FEB*, pp. 46-57.

Revised and expanded between June 2016 and August 2016.

"David McFadden Trip": First published in *A Trip Around McFadden*, ed. Stuart Ross and Jim Smith (Toronto: Front Press/ Proper Tales, 2010), n.pag.

"Plight of the Urban Sasquatch and Other Limericks": Composed from 2010 to 2016—with the exception of "Man from Southampton," which was composed circa 1990-92. "Man from Southampton" was first published in *Unarmed* 61 (n.d.), p. 32.

"Beyond Me": Composed in 2011.

"Incidents of Exposure": Composed on January 1, 2014. First published in *Unarmed* 68 (n.d.), pp. 17-18.

"Some Common and Not-So-Common Similarities": Composed on August 21, 2013. First published in Dusie's "Tuesday Poem" series on September 12, 2017 (www.dusie.blogspot.ca).

"Other News": Composed between November 2015 and August 2016. First published in *The Boat of the Music Is Happy and Diversion* (2017), n.pag.

"Reflection of a Hole": First published in *The Week Shall Inherit the Verse* on November 1, 2012 (www.theweekshallinherittheverse. blogspot.com).

"Distended Aphorisms": First published in *The I.V. Lounge Reader*, ed. Paul Vermeersch (Toronto: Insomniac Press, 2001), pp. 211-12. Included in *FEB*, pp. 72-3.

"Manta Ray Jack and the Crew of the *Spooner*": Included in *FEB*, pp. 74-95. Revised and expanded between June 2016 and April 2017.

GLOSSARY

First published in *VIS*, n.pag.; *SWMPN*, pp. 59-61; and *SA*, pp. 116-19.

# Author's Acknowledgements

Love and thanks to my mother, Marilyn L. Wright, and my sisters, Debra Wright and Sandy Butler, who've supported all my voyages from the start, as had my father, Norman T. Wright (1931-2008); to my first (and last) mate, Dale Zentner, and our wondrous crew: Jesse Huisken, Kerry Zentner, Olia Mishchenko, and Frances Miller; to Charlie Huisken and David Booth, keepers of the familial lighthouses (metaphorically, of course—and yet they do, coincidentally, have real lighthouses, somewhere, I think); to my adventuring brothers-in-law (since well back in the last century), Michael Hurry and Paul Butler, and to all my other relatives at every port from Wrightland to Zentneria; to Wayne Sharpe, Allan Harris, and Randy Loxton, who first set sail with me in 1691...er, 1961, and have been with me through all seas ever since; and to all the ancestors who've now sailed beyond the edge of this world, but who made me what I am today (you know who you are).

Tremendous gratitude and respect to Alessandro Porco, who envisioned and helped manifest this project, and Stuart Ross, who has provided editorial advice on all my texts from the early eighties onward, and has now tailored this material so expertly through his Feed Dog. Fond appreciation as well to Brian Kaufman and friends at Anvil Press, and to the other publishers and editors of my books: Michael Dean, Katy Chan, Clint Burnham, Natalee Caple, Brian Panhuyzen, Darren Wershler, Alana Wilcox, Stan Bevington, and Denis De Klerck; and to all those valued other small-pressers who've marked my words onto everything from tarpaper to Venetian beaches, among them David Owen, Barbara Del Mercato, jwcurry, Nicky Drumbolis, Lillian Necakov, and Nicholas Power.

Thanks also to Clint Hutzulak of Rayola Creative for the cover design; to Richard A. Kirk, William A. Davison and Sherri Lyn Higgins, and Kerry "Sleepy Turbine" Zentner for illustrating earlier volumes; to Lynne Zentner of Long Lake in Mayo, Quebec, for sharing an idyllic landscape where I could become a lake poet for part of each summer, and likewise to Rick/Simon and the other residents of Ward's Island, Toronto (the *Spooner* dropped anchor in both those ports, and wouldn't have been seaworthy without them); to

Jason Camlot for encouragement; to Sarah Moses for proofreading; to Linsey MacPhee for supplying an anecdote that inspired one of the most beautiful "Beautiful Thoughts" thoughts; to Nicky Drumbolis and John Ouzas for suggestions on "Transvocations"; to Paul Dutton for pears and observations; to Dr. Glenn Boggio and Dr. Joseph Marques for tuning and modulation over the years; to the Toronto Arts Council and Ontario Arts Council for financial support during the writing of some of the texts herein; and to all the dedicated printers, binders, booksellers, and reading-series hosts in the Canadian and international small-press communities.

For distending their aphorisms, my apologies to Timothy Leary, Marcus Stellatus Palingenius, Sri Yukteswar, Vladimir Lenin, André Breton, William Shakespeare, Sir Francis Bacon, and the ancient scribes of Iceland.

"Manta Ray Jack and the Crew of the *Spooner*" is an homage to the Reverends Dodgson and Spooner, and Dr. Seuss, too. All spoonerisms (while not necessarily first-discoveries) are originals, apart from five: thanks to Dale Zentner for "the souls in my hawks," Dr. David Naylor for "a word botcher," William A. Davison for "an old guy," and the Rev. William Archibald Spooner himself for his "shoving leopard" and (perhaps apocryphally) "blushing crow."

"The Deregulation of Nature" is dedicated to Christopher Dewdney, whose poetry continues to spring trances upon those willing to ascend and merge.

Sequencing of these texts was conducted at Torpor Vigil Laboratories, Department of Poetry and Other Engineered Texts, Toronto, Ontario, Canada. The author's foretext ("Lighting the Towers") was completed on American National Lighthouse Day 2016. Oh, and—*heiliger bimbam*—happy centennial, DADA!

*Steve Venright*                     Torpor Vigil Industries
venright.com                         torporvigil.com
@stevevenright                       @torporvigil

# Compiler's Acknowledgements

The College of Arts and Sciences at UNCW provided a timely Professional Development Grant that supported a trip to the University of Buffalo's Poetry Collection, allowing me to complete this project. Thanks to Dr. James Maynard, Curator, and the library staff.

Thanks to the many editors and publishers who provided permission to reprint Steve Venright's poetry: Clint Burnham, Natalee Caple, Katy Chan, Denis De Klerck, Paul Dutton, Brian Panhuyzen, and Alana Wilcox.

Thanks to my colleagues in the Department of English at UNCW, especially Nick Crawford, Kate Maddalena, and Jenna McCarthy. To Moez Surani: I am lucky to have your expert advice at the ready. Special thanks to the incomparable Stuart Ross, who enthusiastically supported this project from the very start—and patiently answered my questions with kindness.

Finally, to Steve Venright, who trusted me with this important book many years ago: I am honoured that you've welcomed me into the Hallucinatorium.

*Alessandro Porco*

**Steve Venright** is the author of *Floors of Enduring Beauty* (Mansfield Press, 2007), *Spiral Agitator* (Coach House Books, 2000), *Straunge Wunder; or, The Metalirious Pleasures of Neuralchemy* (Tortoiseshell & Black, 1996), and more. Through his Torpor Vigil Records label, he has released, among other titles, *Dreaming Like Mad with Dion McGregor (Yet More Outrageous Recordings of the World's Most Renowned Sleeptalker)* and Samuel Andreyev's *The Tubular West*. Steve's interest in sensory stimulation and uncommon states of consciousness can be traced to a day in early boyhood when, during a visit to his uncle's farm, he was found happily clutching the electric fence—an experience that foreshadowed his purveying of cranial electrostimulation devices a quarter century later. This fascination also found expression in his travelling Hallucinatorium—a retinal circus sideshow that exploited the psychedelic potential of pulsed-light brain machines—and in the "variegraphic" digitized paintings he has created since 1990. As if inspired by the René Magritte painting *Sixteenth of September*, Steve was born on that date in 1961. At twenty he left his hometown of Sarnia, Ontario, and has resided in Toronto ever since.

**Alessandro Porco** is an Assistant Professor of English at the University of North Carolina, Wilmington. He earned his PhD in Poetics from the State University of New York at Buffalo. He is the editor of the critical edition of Jerrold Levy and Richard Negro's *Poems by Gerard Legro* (Toronto: BookThug, 2016).

THESE CONFLUXIONS WERE MADE OF TEXTOPLASM
TO RESEMBLE HUMAN THOUGHT